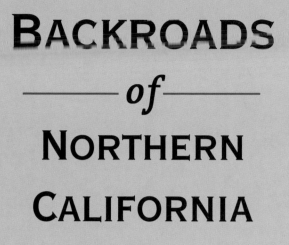

BACKROADS

—of—

NORTHERN CALIFORNIA

YOUR GUIDE TO
NORTHERN CALIFORNIA'S
MOST SCENIC BACKROAD TOURS

David M. Wyman

Voyageur Press

A Pictorial
Discovery Guide

Edited by Todd R. Berger
Designed by Kristy Tucker and Andrea Rud
Cover designed by Kristy Tucker
Printed in Hong Kong

04   05   6   5   4   3

Library of Congress Cataloging-in-Publication Data
Wyman, David M., 1948–
    Backroads of Northern California : your guide to Northern California's most scenic
      backroad tours / David M. Wyman.
        p. cm. — (A pictorial discovery guide)
    Includes bibliographical references (p. 156) and index.
    ISBN 0-89658-482-8 (alk. paper) — ISBN 0-89658-407-0 (pbk. : alk. paper)
      1. California, Northern—Tours. 2. Automobile travel—California,
Northern—Guidebooks. 3. Scenic byways—California, Northern—Guidebooks.
4. California, Northern—Pictorial works. I. Title. II. Series.

F867.5.W96 2000
917.94—dc21   99-046003

Distributed in Canada by Raincoast Books, 9050 Shaughnessy Street, Vancouver, B.C. V6P 6E5

Published by Voyageur Press, Inc.
123 North Second Street, P.O. Box 338, Stillwater, MN 55082 U.S.A.
651-430-2210, fax 651-430-2211
books@voyageurpress.com
www.voyageurpress.com

Educators, fundraisers, premium and gift buyers, publicists, and marketing managers: Looking for creative products and new sales ideas? Voyageur Press books are available at special discounts when purchased in quantities, and special editions can be created to your specifications. For details contact the marketing department at 800-888-9653.

PAGE 1:
HIGHWAY 108 WINDING TOWARD SONORA PASS AND THE CREST OF THE TOWERING SIERRA NEVADA.

PAGE 2:
AN AUTUMN RAINSTORM IN LATE AFTERNOON CLEARS OVER THE BEAR RIVER RIDGE ROAD IN THE COAST RANGES ALONG THE LOST COAST.

PAGE 3, INSET:
A DISK MACHINE, USED TO FURROW THE SOIL, SITS IDLY FOR NOW, ON A FARM NEAR MANTECA.

FACING PAGE:
AN OLD-TIME GAS PUMP SITS IN RETIREMENT NEAR HIGHWAY 49 IN GOLD RUSH COUNTRY.

DEDICATION

To my parents, who passed on their wanderlust to me

ACKNOWLEDGMENTS

Thanks first and foremost go to my wife, Kathy Burke, who spent many days traveling with me from dawn to dusk, sometimes going without coffee in the morning and driving while I made my notes. She also put up with my long absences when I wasn't home to take the kids to school or to take out the garbage.

I would also like to thank the people at Voyageur Press who put their faith in me to complete a task that at times I thought might prove too daunting to accomplish. In particular, I owe much to Todd Berger, who edited the text.

Friends Lori Sweeney and Kate Dumont generously helped me edit some of the text early on in the writing of this book. Irene Shibata provided invaluable resource material.

For their encouragement, inspiration, and connections, I thank David Anderson and Randy Leffingwell.

Reid Bogert served, with much good humor, as my travel companion on several trips. He was tireless as a driver. Duane Babinski, Bob Bernardo, Larry Hernandez, Bill Porter, Jim Valensi, Kirsten "Kit" Blaemire, Silas Lum, Richard Nolthenius, and Jim Rosenberg accompanied me on additional trips.

Several local historians, including Clarence Chu, Bob Hines, Jan Holman, Alice Jones, Scott Lawson, Ronnie Maiden, Lois McDonald, Steve Moore, Byron Nelson, John Nople, Lonnie Patterson, Leroy Radanovich, and Evelyn Whisman, read portions of my manuscript and offered suggestions. Mike Clynne, with the U.S. Geological Survey; Jim Rock, an archeologist with the U.S. Forest Service; and Nancy Bailey, with Lassen Volcanic National Park, also read portions of my manuscript and helped make some corrections. Hupa tribal archivist Leslie Campbell, and Ellen Harding, with the California State Library, helped me find historic photographs.

Thanks, also, go to my dog, Beau, who was a faithful companion on many of my sojourns around Northern California.

FACING PAGE: THE FLOODED AFTERMATH OF A RAINSTORM ON A COUNTRY ROAD WEST OF FRESNO.

CONTENTS

A FARMSTEAD HIGH IN THE MOUNTAINS ABOVE THE LOST COAST, WEST OF THE LUMBER TOWNS OF SCOTIA AND RIO DELL.

DOOR AND FLOWERS IN THE DELTA TOWN OF LOCKE AT THE SOUTH END OF MAIN STREET.

THE BRIDGEPORT COVERED BRIDGE SPANS THE SOUTH YUBA RIVER, JUST WEST OF PLEASANT VALLEY ROAD.

INTRODUCTION

I remember Sunday excursions with my family when I was a child. Sitting between my grandparents, I would peer out the backseat windows, or I would argue with my little brother while we explored what was, at that time, rural land in Southern California. My dad drove along two-lane country roads where the speed limit was never more than fifty-five miles an hour.

A few years later my parents extended those excursions, taking my brother and me into the northern part of the state during summer vacations. We drove through the rich farmlands and the little towns of the Central Valley, along the east side of the Sierra Nevada Mountains, and through the fringes of the Great Basin Desert. We traveled through Gold Country, watched black bears raid trash cans in Yosemite National Park, and boated over the pristine waters of Lake Tahoe.

Still later, I attended college in Northern California. While there, I wrote about and photographed the local backroads for the campus newspaper. If I learned anything in college, it was an appreciation of the land and history of the northern half of the state.

Those early experiences explain why I still feel a sense of excitement whenever I travel around the Golden State, whether I'm in a car, on my bike, or on foot. And they explain my criteria for exploring the

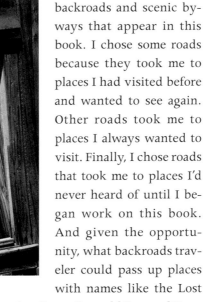

backroads and scenic byways that appear in this book. I chose some roads because they took me to places I had visited before and wanted to see again. Other roads took me to places I always wanted to visit. Finally, I chose roads that took me to places I'd never heard of until I began work on this book. And given the opportunity, what backroads traveler could pass up places with names like the Lost Coast, Roaring Camp, Emerald Bay, and Paradise?

Deciding on the tours for this book was the easy part. I had more difficulty settling on a theme. I proudly began telling friends and family I was working on a book about scenic byways, and, inevitably, each person would ask, "What's the book about?" For a while, even I wasn't sure.

Eventually, it became clear. This book isn't about highway numbers and compass directions, although there are plenty of each to be found in these pages. This book isn't a definitive volume on history, geology, or geography. Nor does this book cover every backroad and scenic byway in Northern California; such a gargantuan undertaking needs more than one volume.

This is, I came to understand, a book about legends and myths, about history and the landscape. Like tapestries of tightly woven yarn, the stories in this book are woven

together by the backroads of Northern California. There are stories here about streets paved with gold, a river in the desert deep enough to float a ship, monsters of the deep, primordial creatures of the forest, and elephants of the Sierra Nevada foothills. There are tales about mountains that have moved across a great valley and mountains borne of fire and ice. There are stories of mountain men, pioneer women, the man who wanted to build the world's biggest telescope, and the tintinnabulations made by the world's master bell makers. The backroads, then, are simply the tools that allow us to travel through time and space, between myth and reality, on a journey through the Golden State.

I also had to give some consideration to the question of where Northern California begins, at least on its southern border. It was no good asking for advice. Some people told me the dividing line begins well north of San Francisco. Others assured me that Northern California begins just over the northern border of Los Angeles.

Such opinions aside, there is in fact a symbolic, living dividing point for the state, near the city of Fresno in the Central Valley. There, two trees sit next to each other on the median strip along an otherwise anonymous stretch of California Highway 99. The tree to the north is a pine, the tree to the south is a palm, and both are equidistant from the Oregon and Mexico borders. If we could stretch an imaginary line between those trees to the east of Fresno, it would run through Yosemite and over the Sierra Nevada Mountains. The line would continue into the Great Basin Desert at the Nevada border. Extend the line west of Fresno, and it would climb over the Coast Ranges and touch the Pacific Ocean at the town of Santa Cruz. Imaginary though it may be, this line will serve as the dividing line for this book.

The land north of the line is vast and complex. Geologically cataclysmic events in the distant and recent past have played important roles in shaping the physical features of the state. Topographically, the land reaches from sea level to more than fourteen thousand feet. There is an enormous river delta and a vast desert, as well as the longest mountain range in North America and the shortest mountain range in the world.

The human history of the north is no less complex, created by the interactions—sometimes peaceful, sometimes violent—of many peoples. Native Americans were first to arrive around ten thousand years ago. They were followed much later by Spanish soldiers and priests, by British and Russian fur trappers, and, from the United States, by mountain men and soldiers. During the epic California gold rush, people from around the world swarmed into Northern California. Where people have come, the roads—from footpaths to superhighways—have followed.

In organizing this book, I divided the northern part of the state into several somewhat arbitrary regions. The divisions overlap in geography, geology, and history. Even the roads overlap at times. But if there are some regional similarities, there are even more differences. The Coast Ranges region is defined on the most obvious level by its relationship with the Pacific Ocean, and the area contains some of the state's finest groves of giant redwoods along its backroads and byways. The rugged Klamath Mountains dominate the northwest part of California, while the Central Valley is the agricultural heartland of the state. In the vast Sacramento Delta, thirteen of California's rivers coalesce into one. The Cascades embrace California's great mountains borne of fire and ice. The Great Basin Desert, the largest desert in the United States, averages no more than twelve inches of rain each year, yet can accumulate several feet of snow over the course of a single winter. The Sierra Nevada Mountains are rich with gold rush history and high country scenery. And finally, the wine country, a diverse region of vineyards and mountains fermented in California's cultural and political history.

To help me explore the roads in this book, I employed a number of maps and atlases. The *California Road Atlas and Driver's Guide*, published by Thomas Brothers, is an invaluable resource, showing every state and county road I traveled. I also used the *Northern California Atlas and Gazetteer*, published by DeLorme, which provides detailed topographic maps. I stocked up on a large collection of excellent county and regional maps from AAA, and I had numerous county and chamber of commerce maps, which I often picked up during the course of my travels. I also relied on National Park Service and National Forest Service maps, which are particularly useful for accurately showing unpaved roads.

Even when I thought I knew exactly where I was going, I made an effort to find a "local" to ask directions. More than once someone provided me with a tip about a new road, an impassable road that would be best to avoid, or interesting local history that I wouldn't have gleaned from a map or a book. While talking to a stranger can be a little intimidating, it can also be a quick way to make a friend. I've made many friends while working on this project.

I've driven all the roads described in this book. A few gravel roads are always so listed. All of the roads can be navigated by an ordinary passenger car, minivan, or pickup truck.

That said, I carried a spare tire, a foot pump, and a first-aid kit whenever I went on the road. I never needed a shovel, but I did carry one. Although I rarely brought much in the way of tools, I did make use of my trusty Swiss Army knife and a mini Leatherman pocket tool, which let me tighten screws on my camera, open a wine bottle, and replace the brake lights.

It was so easy to be seduced by the siren call of new roads that I was never sure where I would conclude my day. So I stowed a sleeping bag and foam pad in my car, even when I carried a credit card and had a confirmed motel reservation. When traveling in the mountains during winter and spring, I carried tire chains, and I needed them a few times.

I apologize in advance if I've failed to include someone's favorite road in this book. My intent here is simple: to travel down two-lane country roads, where the speed limit is never more than fifty-five miles per hour.

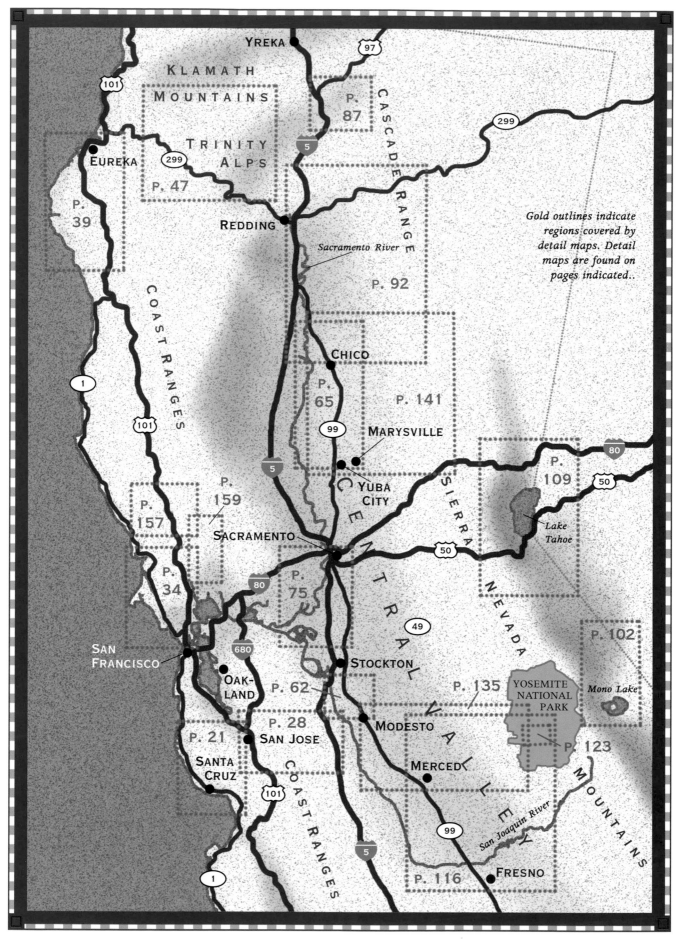

YREKA

KLAMATH

MOUNTAINS

97

101

P.
87

299

TRINITY
ALPS

299

EUREKA

P. 47

CASCADE RANGE

P.
39

REDDING

Sacramento River

*Gold outlines indicate
regions covered by
detail maps. Detail
maps are found on
pages indicated..*

P. 92

COAST RANGES

CHICO

P.
65

P. 141

1

101

99

MARYSVILLE

80

P.
109

50

YUBA
CITY

*Lake
Tahoe*

5

P.
159

P.
157

SACRAMENTO

SIERRA NEVADA

P.
34

80

P.
75

50

P. 102

49

Mono Lake

SAN
FRANCISCO

680

STOCKTON

CENTRAL VALLEY

YOSEMITE
NATIONAL
PARK

OAK-
LAND

P. 62

P. 135

P. 28

MODESTO

MOUNTAINS

P. 21

SAN JOSE

P. 123

SANTA
CRUZ

MERCED

101

San Joaquin River

COAST RANGES

1

99

5

P. 116

FRESNO

ABOVE:
EARLY MORNING LIGHT
ILLUMINATES THE
GLACIERS AND SNOW-
FIELDS THAT COVER THE
DORMANT MOUNT
SHASTA VOLCANO,
VIEWED FROM THE
NORTH ON MILITARY
PASS ROAD.

LEFT:
MAIN STREET IN THE
SLEEPY DELTA TOWN OF
LOCKE.

OVERLEAF:
DAWN OVER MOUNT
TALLAC AND TAYLOR
MARSH, VIEWED FROM
THE SOUTH SHORE OF
LAKE TAHOE.

PART I

THE
COAST RANGES

Like a leviathan risen from the deep, the Coast Ranges stand guard over the western edge of North America, stretching (within California) from the Oregon border in the north to the city of Santa Barbara in the south.

Over millions of years these frequently misty mountains have been lifted thousands of feet above the level of the sea. As the Coast Ranges rose, their western slopes were chiseled into a series of giant steps, or terraces, by the pounding of waves against the shore. Most of the coastal mountains have five to seven terraces, some easy to spot on rocky headlands, others more indistinct because they are covered by trees and plants. But each terrace, even if covered by vegetation, can still be detected. That's because each terrace has its own zone of vegetation.

For many visitors to the Coast Ranges, the most interesting zone of vegetation is on the second terrace, about a mile back and two hundred feet up from the sea. This is the zone of the coastal redwoods, the tallest trees in the world, which can reach a height of 365 feet, and can live for two thousand years. The redwoods require enormous amounts of moisture, and they get what they need from an average of forty to sixty inches of rainfall per year in their vegetation zone. Abundant fog, created when the air above the relatively warm water of the Pacific mixes with the colder air over coastal water, will precipitate an additional twelve inches of moisture.

The western slopes of the Coast Ranges block the rain and fog from the eastern slopes, which face the Central Valley. The woodlands on the interior side of the mountains support oaks and pines, trees well adapted to drier country. Grasslands beneath the trees have been converted to pastures and, increasingly, to vineyards.

U.S. Highway 101 runs the length of the Coast Ranges, along the Pacific and in the river valleys of the western slopes. Except for its intermittent stretches of four-lane freeway, U.S. 101 would deserve notable inclusion in this book. On the eastern side, Interstate 5 parallels the Coast Ranges.

The trio of roads covered in these pages explore more remote country. Two tours travel through groves of redwoods on opposite ends of the Coast Ranges, while a third climbs east of the San Francisco Bay Area to crest the mountains.

INSET:
A WHALE SCULPTURE GRACES A FRONT PORCH RAILING AT POINT REYES STATION, SOUTH OF TOMALES BAY.

FACING PAGE:
THE LICK OBSERVATORY FROM ONE OF THE MANY SWITCHBACKS ON THE MOUNT HAMILTON ROAD.

THE SANTA CRUZ MOUNTAINS

Although the main route from Santa Cruz to the Bay Area is over busy California Highway 17, other roads offer scenic alternatives into the beautiful Santa Cruz Mountains. The following tours link three state parks and thousands of coastal redwoods, an old-fashioned steam engine and a covered bridge, a backroad that's not for the faint of heart, and migrating whales.

California Highway 9 to Henry Cowell Redwoods State Park

Santa Cruz sits on the northern edge of Monterey Bay and on the southern edge of the Santa Cruz Mountains. The land had been long settled by the Ohlone, before the arrival of the Spanish in 1774. Seventeen years later, the Spaniards founded a mission at Santa Cruz.

Highway 9 leads north from Santa Cruz along the western bank of the San Lorenzo River. A sign warns of curves ahead as the highway begins to ascend the western slopes of the river canyon and enters a forest of Douglas fir, madrone, and oaks. About five miles from Santa Cruz, the canyon walls begin to widen and Highway 9 reaches the southern unit of Henry Cowell Redwoods State Park, which is on the outskirts of the little town of Felton, at the bottom of the San Lorenzo Valley.

The land for the park was donated to the state by Samuel Cowell, the last surviving child of Henry Cowell. The elder Cowell came to California from Massachusetts during the gold rush and made his fortune, not as a miner, but as a businessman. Cowell made enough money to purchase extensive property in several areas, including in San Francisco and in the Santa Cruz Mountains. He also owned the land that is now the site of the University of California at Santa Cruz—a place where protection of the redwoods and the spectacular views of the mountains are considered to be the most important elements of the campus landscape.

The southern unit of Henry Cowell Redwoods State Park features a campground (accessible from Graham Hill Road) and fifteen miles of hiking and riding trails. The half-mile-long, self-guided Circle Trail wanders through a grove of two-thousand-year-old redwoods, and starts just a few yards from the park's nature center. Keep an eye out for the banana slug, a slimy mollusk that also serves as the U.C. Santa Cruz mascot.

The Roaring Camp and Big Trees Narrow Gauge Railroad is adjacent to the state park, within a few hundred yards of the nature center. The steam-powered trains at Roaring Camp, which began transporting lumber out of the mountains in 1875, now carry passengers each summer, offering loop rides through the redwood forest, or trips back and forth to Santa Cruz.

The San Lorenzo Valley

Although it's easy to walk to the train depot from the state park, the auto entrance is in Felton, off of Graham Hill Road (named for Isaac Graham, a prominent logger and moonshiner in the mid-nineteenth century).

Felton once served the timber and limestone industries. Now Felton and the other towns in the San Lorenzo Valley cater to tourists and house residents who often work in the Bay Area on the far side of the mountains.

Felton is justifiably proud of its covered bridge, which spans the tree-shaded San Lorenzo River just north of the state park and Roaring Camp. Although the original bridge, built in 1892, was destroyed by floodwaters in the 1980s, its replacement is an exact replica, and, from roadway to roof, is the tallest covered bridge in the United States. Closed to motorized traffic, the bridge offers a footpath to Henry Cowell and Roaring Camp.

At Felton, Highway 9 crosses the Felton Empire Road, which cuts west near the southern end of Fall Creek. This area is the northern unit of Henry Cowell Redwoods State Park, with 2,390 acres of parkland and

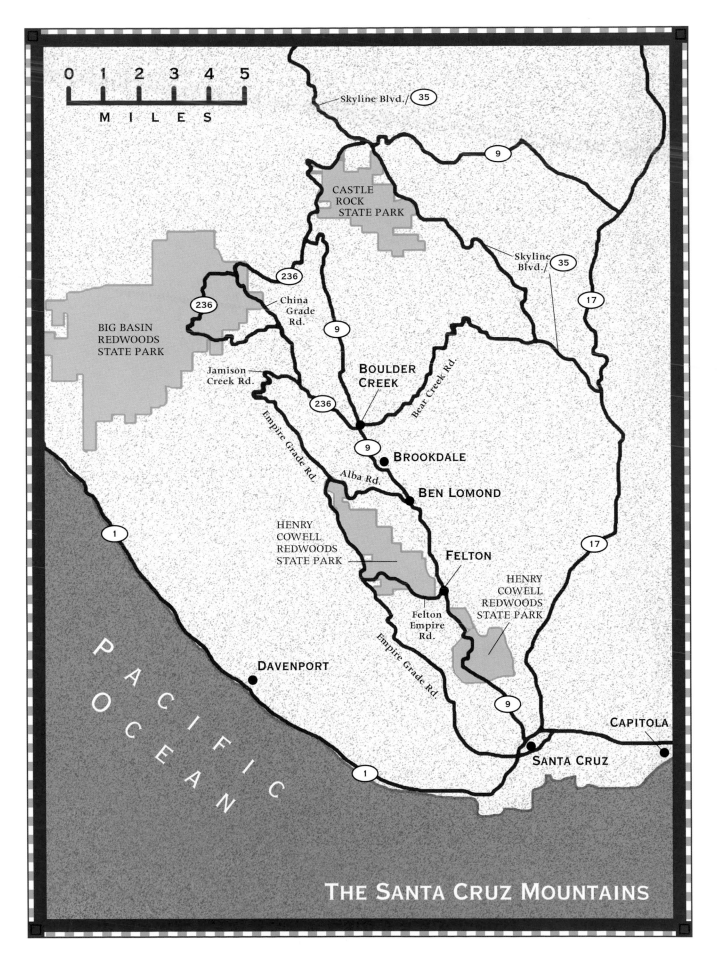

0 1 2 3 4 5

MILES

Skyline Blvd. / 35

9

CASTLE ROCK STATE PARK

Skyline Blvd. / 35

17

236

236

China Grade Rd.

BIG BASIN REDWOODS STATE PARK

9

BOULDER CREEK

Bear Creek Rd.

Jamison Creek Rd.

236

9

BROOKDALE

Empire Grade Rd.

Alba Rd.

BEN LOMOND

HENRY COWELL REDWOODS STATE PARK

FELTON

17

HENRY COWELL REDWOODS STATE PARK

1

Felton Empire Rd.

Empire Grade Rd.

DAVENPORT

9

PACIFIC OCEAN

CAPITOLA

1

SANTA CRUZ

THE SANTA CRUZ MOUNTAINS

more than twenty miles of trails that follow old wagon and logging roads. Some trails lead to the ruins of kilns once operated by the Cowell family. The kilns heated limestone that was dug out of the local mountains and used to make lime, which, when mixed with sand and water, could be used as building plaster. After the great San Francisco Earthquake of 1906, Cowell's limestone was used to help rebuild the ruined city.

North of Felton, Highway 9 continues through the little community of Ben Lomond, named after the mountain towering above it. Ben Lomond was originally founded as a logging town, but by the early 1900s it had turned into a summer resort

center for the wealthy. A little past Ben Lomond, Alba Road skirts the northern end of Fall Creek, and offers access, via Empire Grade Road and Jamison Creek Road, to California Highway 236 and Big Basin Redwoods State Park.

At Brookdale, just north of Ben Lomond on Highway 9, watch for a thirty-foot-high mural of actor James Dean on the west side of the road. The mural graces the side of the Brookdale Lodge, once the exclusive haunt of the rich and famous; today, it is said to be haunted by ghosts. Need another reason to stop? Enjoy a meal beside a natural brook that runs through the lodge's dining room.

Like Ben Lomond, the town of Boulder Creek (a little further along Highway 9) started out as a logging camp in the 1860s. It quickly became one of the state's busiest and wildest logging towns with a number of saloons—and brothels. These days it's a lot quieter, but remains very picturesque. If you're still hungry, try Adelita's, a terrific Mexican restaurant perched next to the river.

LEFT, TOP:
A FENCE OF STACKED REDWOOD LOGS GUARDS A PRIVATE RESIDENCE ALONG EMPIRE GRADE ROAD.

LEFT, BOTTOM:
THE COVERED BRIDGE OVER THE SAN LORENZO AT FELTON ON A SPRING DAY.

FACING PAGE:
COASTAL REDWOODS IN HENRY COWELL REDWOODS STATE PARK.

Beyond Boulder Creek

From Boulder Creek, Highway 9 begins to climb steeply into the Santa Cruz Mountains, leaving the river valley and civilization behind. Redwoods line the north-facing portions of the road, while oaks and Douglas fir grow on dryer slopes. After seven miles, the road reaches Highway 236 where a left turn leads to Big Basin Redwoods State Park. We'll take the right turn, which keeps us on Highway 9, heading toward Castle Rock State Park. Watch along the road for poppies and lupine in spring and early summer growing on sunny, open slopes. Occasional pullouts along this stretch of the road offer views of the forested mountains marching off toward the distant sea.

After six miles, Highway 236 circles back to again intersect Highway 9, which meanders a few miles farther north to California Highway 35. Also known as Skyline Boulevard, Highway 35 offers access to the Bay Area as well as busy Highway 17 and Santa Cruz. For an interesting route back to Boulder Creek, turn right (south) on Skyline. Trailhead parking for Castle Rock State Park is just past the intersection. The park features unusual rock formations, creeks and waterfalls, thirty-two miles of wilderness hiking trails, and more than three thousand acres of mostly wilderness terrain.

From the park, it's about seven miles to Bear Creek Road, which winds down through ten miles of oaks, madrones, and redwoods, and past a succession of wineries and vineyards before reaching Boulder Creek.

California Highway 236 to Big Basin Redwoods State Park

From Boulder Creek, Highway 236 travels northwest for about ten miles to Big Basin Redwoods State Park, the oldest state park in California. The park was created early in the twentieth century to save the dwindling numbers of redwoods, which, unlike their cousins in the Sierra Nevada Mountains, were commercially logged. If you visit the park in spring or summer, look at the side of the road for lupine and huckleberry; the latter is a tall bush with bunches of purple berries. And plenty of mushrooms grow in the moist soil along forest trails.

In addition to the largest contiguous grove of coastal redwoods in the state, the eighteen thousand acres at Big Basin contain campgrounds, tent cabins, picnic spots, and trails for those on foot and horseback. The Redwood Trail, opposite the visitor center, is about a half mile long and offers a good introduction to the park. Other, far more ambitious trails lead for many miles, northeast to Castle Rock State Park, and west to the sea.

After visiting the park, you can continue on Highway 236 to reach Castle Rock State Park via Highway 9 and Skyline Boulevard. Just before reaching the Castle Rock State Park boundary, however, Highway 236 intersects the China Grade Road and provides an alternate backroad to explore. Be prepared to make a steep descent through the forest; the road follows the course of Boulder Creek, which drops through a narrow canyon choked with redwoods and madrones. At the bottom of the canyon the road passes over a one-lane bridge to reach a residential area at Foxglove Lane. Highway 236 is then regained about halfway between the Big Basin visitor center and Boulder Creek.

Capitola and Davenport

The town of Capitola, which bills itself as the first beach resort in California, is three miles south of Santa Cruz. Built in the late 1800s, Capitola attracted people from the Central Valley seeking to escape the summer heat. Capitola features an abundance of Victorian-era summer cottages and homes, as well as narrow, picturesque streets.

One of the early residents of Capitola was whaling captain John Davenport. In 1868 Davenport and his family moved from Capitola to a spot about nine miles north of Santa Cruz, where Davenport built a 450-foot wharf. Soon Davenport, the town that sprouted around the wharf, became a thriv-

LEFT:
MY FRIEND KIT BLAEMIRE WHEELS HER VAN ALONG THE CHINA GRADE ROAD NEAR BIG BASIN REDWOODS STATE PARK.

BELOW:
A REDWOOD TOWERS OVER THE ROOF OF THE VISITOR CENTER AT BIG BASIN REDWOODS STATE PARK.

ing community where timber, cordwood, and cedar posts were loaded onto small sailing vessels and shipped to San Francisco.

Whaling expeditions also departed from Davenport; whaling gear and blubber melting pots were located near the pier. Today, the whales are no longer hunted by men with harpoons. Instead, Davenport is a good place to watch for migrating gray whales in winter and spring as they make their way up and down the coast.

THE MOUNT HAMILTON ROAD

One blustery day in mid-spring, when the sun danced in and out of gray clouds that covered most of the heavens, I climbed onto my bicycle and began the long ascent up the Mount Hamilton Road. I was on my way to visit the Lick Observatory, high in the Diablo Range above the city of San Jose and the Santa Clara Valley. Contained within the great domed vault of the Main Building is one of the world's largest refractor telescopes. Beneath the telescope itself is the crypt of the man who was responsible for the construction of the observatory.

Journey toward the Heavens

To reach the Lick Observatory, exit off either U.S. 101 or Interstate 680 in San Jose at Alum Rock Avenue, and go east to the Mount Hamilton Road, which is also California Highway 130. The lower reaches of the route pass through a residential neighborhood of luxury homes, but the narrow road soon offers encompassing views to the south and southwest. The scenery becomes more rural as the highway climbs over and around steep slopes of oak forests and grasslands, with the Santa Clara Valley and the Bay Area stretching out below like a giant relief map.

On my bike ride there were, to my dismay, only two downhill sections. The first is a mile and a half or so up the mountain at Joseph D. Grant County Park, and the second is some miles farther at Smith Creek, where a hotel and restaurant once stood. This is also where the road begins to

switchback in earnest. At long last I came around a sharp bend and spotted the dome of the Main Building, though my destination was far above me; scores of switchbacks still lay ahead. I peddled on, winding my way ever closer to the summit.

Atop Mount Hamilton

When I finally reached the enormous, white-domed Lick Observatory, I peered back down the eighteen miles of road I'd just climbed. Even on this hazy, cloudy day, the blue waters of San Francisco Bay were visible far to the northwest and forty-two hundred vertical feet below the top of the mountain. Behind the Main Building, another

ABOVE:
ONE OF THE MANY PICTURESQUE MANSIONS AT CAPITOLA.

FACING PAGE:
A CREEK FLOWS PAST MOSS-COVERED ROCKS AT CASTLE ROCK STATE PARK.

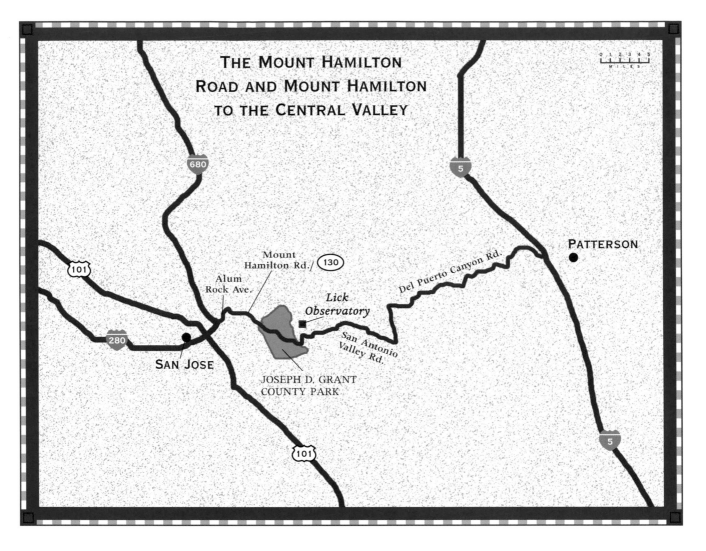

THE MOUNT HAMILTON
ROAD AND MOUNT HAMILTON
TO THE CENTRAL VALLEY

PATTERSON

huge dome housed the 120-inch Shane Telescope. Other domes were scattered around the mountain, along with maintenance buildings and private residences. A sign on a dormitory behind the Main Building warned that astronomers were sleeping. There were wonderful views of the Diablo Range to the north and south.

Mount Hamilton was named for the Reverend Laurentine Hamilton, a Bay Area minister. In August 1861, Hamilton climbed the peak with two companions who were carrying surveying gear. The unencumbered Hamilton reached the summit first and called out, perhaps a bit boastfully, "First on top!"

The Lick Observatory was named for the man who brought it into being. James Lick was one of the more eccentric characters in the history of California. Born in 1796 in Fredericksburg, Pennsylvania, Lick initially earned his living making and selling pianos

and organs. In 1820 he moved to Buenos Aires, Argentina, apparently continuing in the same business. Returning to North America, Lick arrived in San Francisco sometime around the beginning of 1848. He must have done well in South America, because he reportedly brought with him an iron chest that contained what was worth $30,000 (in mid-nineteenth century dollars) in gold doubloons. Through real estate investments, Lick parlayed that fortune into one worth $3 million, purchasing property in the center of San Francisco, the Santa Clara Valley, and in southern California.

In the spring of 1873, Lick decided that he wanted to fund the construction of a telescope "larger and more powerful than any existing," as a fitting monument to his life, as he saw it.

Lick gave some $700,000 to build the Lick Telescope, with the operation of the

observatory to be consigned to the University of California. Up to that time, no observatory had been built in the mountains. Astronomers had not yet realized the importance of night skies unpolluted by the artificial light created by cities, although Isaac Newton had suggested the benefit of high altitude night sky observations in 1717.

Lick, in fact, wanted his telescope built in downtown San Francisco, but was convinced to find a suitable location in the mountains. Sites were considered in the Sierra Nevada Mountains, as well as in Wyoming and Colorado. Mount Hamilton was chosen in 1875 because of its high elevation and because San Jose was close enough to make building and supplying the observatory relatively easy.

The construction of the Lick Observatory, which began in 1880, took eight years. Workers blasted thirty feet off the top of the

ABOVE:

LOOKING DOWN THE OAK-DOTTED HILLS AND THE SWITCHBACKS OF MOUNT HAMILTON ROAD FROM THE LICK OBSERVATORY.

LEFT:

A VIEW OF THE RURAL LANDSCAPE ALONG A LOWER STRETCH OF THE MOUNT HAMILTON ROAD.

mountain, moving forty thousand tons of rock to level the site. They also constructed the Mount Hamilton Road at a grade of five to six percent, gentle enough to allow teams of horses to haul all the heavy materials up the mountain.

Near the summit, masons built a kiln next to a bed of clay, where they fired bricks for the buildings. In the dome of the Main Building, the movable floor—sixty feet in diameter—was designed so it could be raised or lowered a distance of sixteen and one-half feet, in synchronization with the eye-piece end of the telescope. Sixteen and one-half feet is the distance the eyepiece end can swing as it moves up and down, sweeping the night sky in search of heavenly bodies. Without a movable floor, an astronomer would need to climb up and down a ladder to stay with the eyepiece as the telescope was adjusted. The eyepiece end of the telescope can also swing back and forth horizontally.

The first telescope to be built was the Lick Telescope, a big, 36-inch refractor telescope. Like a spyglass, a refractor telescope uses a clear glass lens to bend, or refract, light rays to form an image. The Lick Telescope was the largest the world had yet seen. Less than ten years later, the University of Chicago built the Yerkes Observatory in southeastern Wisconsin, which featured a 40-inch refractor, still the largest in the world, because any refractor larger than that

size will slump and deform under its own weight.

Soon additional telescopes and scientific apparatus joined the big, 36-inch refractor telescope. Today, four other telescopes, including the 120-inch Shane reflector, grace the mountaintop. The barrels of reflecting telescopes, which use mirrors, are much shorter than refractor barrels. The 120-inch Shane reflector and the 36-inch Lick refractor telescopes, for example, are housed in domes that are almost identical in size, even though the Shane Telescope has eleven times the light-gathering power of the Lick Telescope.

Astronomers and their families followed the telescopes, and an elementary school was built by 1900. By the 1960s, the population on Mount Hamilton reached almost one hundred.

The Main Building of the Lick Observatory, which houses the 36-inch telescope and a gift shop, is open to visitors most of the year, except when winter ice and snow close the road. On my visit to the observatory, I took an informative tour of the Main Building, which included a look at the Lick Telescope.

One man who never visited the observatory was James Lick. Nor did he even visit the summit of Mount Hamilton, at least during his lifetime. Lick died on October 1, 1876, at the age of eighty, four years before construction of the observatory and telescope even began. Lick did eventually make the journey up the mountain in 1887, when his remains were placed at the base of his great telescope. A bronze tablet marks his resting place.

After my tour, I climbed back onto my bike and coasted down the mountain the way I'd come, a fitting reward for my efforts.

MOUNT HAMILTON TO THE CENTRAL VALLEY

The road from San Jose to Mount Hamilton does not end at the Lick Observatory. Instead, it can be savored for an additional fifty, mostly convoluted miles. Alternately

THE MAIN BUILDING, INCLUDING THE DOME CONTAINING THE 120-INCH REFRACTOR TELESCOPE, AT THE LICK OBSERVATORY.

offering panoramic views of the high country and plunging into deep canyons, the route follows the footsteps of sixteenth-century Spanish explorers and nineteenth-century American scientists, before terminating in the Central Valley.

Beyond the Summit

On another trip up the Mount Hamilton Road, this time behind the wheel of a car, I drove past the observatory to explore the eastern side of the mountains. Once over the summit, the terrain becomes far steeper and hillier than the slopes on the western side. Still listed as Highway 130, the Mount Hamilton Road becomes the San Antonio Valley Road, a road that feels like a roller coaster ride, dropping off one pine-covered ridge and rising up another. But the road bucks steadily downward, eventually dropping a few hundred feet in elevation, and the pines begin to share the landscape with oaks and chaparral.

Explorer William Brewer is well known for his expeditions into the Sierra Nevada Mountains; in fact, he named the highest peak in California Mount Whitney (after Josiah Dwight Whitney, who directed the

LEFT, TOP:
THE JUNCTION, A COUNTRY STORE AT A SPLIT IN THE ROAD, WITH THE BAY AREA DOWN ONE SIDE OF THE MOUNTAIN AND THE CENTRAL VALLEY DOWN THE OTHER.

LEFT, BOTTOM:
MAILBOXES, COUNTRY-STYLE, ALONG SAN ANTONIO VALLEY ROAD.

California Geological Survey in the early 1860s). Brewer also explored the mountains around Mount Hamilton. He wrote it "is almost a terra-incognita. No map represents it, no explorers touch it."

However, the Spanish had explored the mountains long before Brewer. In 1776, frontiersman and army officer Juan Bautista de Anza and his soldiers found the terrain so rugged that the troops called the area *Sierra de Chasco*, "the mountains that played a joke." Later, the rugged mountains became known as the Diablos, the Devil's range.

The Junction

Continuing along the San Antonio Valley Road, I rounded a bend and saw two bobcats sitting next to each other on the edge of the pavement. I have a feeling I was more surprised to see them than they were to see me. They nonchalantly watched my car slow almost to a halt before they finally ran off. One of the two disappeared into the chaparral, while the other bobcat climbed up a tall oak tree and calmly peered down at me, looking like an enormous, spotted house cat. This kitty sported black tufts at the ends of its long ears and the trademark bobbed tail.

About seventeen miles past the Lick Observatory, the terrain gradually levels out. Here, the road, lined with oaks strewn with mistletoe and Spanish moss, passes through the San Antonio Valley.

At the far end of the San Antonio Valley the road splits. To the left, Mines Road drops down a canyon and ends in Livermore, back on the west side of the mountains. To the right, Del Puerto Canyon Road twists and turns thirty-one more miles down to Interstate 5, on the west side of the Central Valley. At the split in the road, a country store called The Junction welcomes travelers. It is the only place for thirty miles in any direction where people can shop for groceries, eat a hamburger, or have a beer.

A bookmobile put in its once a month appearance the day I stopped at The Junction. Over the next hour perhaps a dozen cars pulled into the parking lot. People returned their borrowed books and videos and checked out new ones, then popped into The Junction for groceries or a cup of coffee or just to say hello.

Down Del Puerto

From The Junction, the route to the Central Valley leads torturously down Del Puerto Canyon. At first, much of the terrain is both steep and narrow as the road follows the twisting path of Del Puerto Creek. Then the canyon broadens and reaches Frank Raines Park, named for a Stanislaus County supervisor who served from 1917 until 1953. The park contains roughly two thousand acres, with a campground, picnic area, and hiking trails. More than a quarter of the park is reserved for off-road vehicle use.

Past the park the road narrows again, staying high for a time above the south side of the creek. The pines give way entirely to oaks now, and the road drops down to the canyon bottom where horses browse and cavort on the open pastureland. The road climbs one last time, then contours around gently rolling hills before it descends into the Central Valley and meets Interstate 5. Traffic on the interstate rushes north toward the San Francisco Bay Area and Sacramento, and south toward Los Angeles, along the western edge of the Central Valley.

California Highway 33, a few miles to the east of the interstate, offers a more relaxed alternative. Highway 33 travels through little agricultural towns like Crows Landing and Gustine to the south, and Westley to the north. Farther north, Highway 33 reaches California Highway 132, offering scenic routes to Modesto and Manteca covered elsewhere in this book.

TOMALES BAY AND CALIFORNIA HIGHWAY 1

Tomales Bay is overlooked by many visitors who stop just south at the more well known Point Reyes National Seashore. But Tomales Bay, in Marin County (about thirty-five miles north of San Francisco on Highway 1), is a worthy destination in its own right, with quaint villages, natural areas thriving with wildlife, and a beautiful landscape shaped by the seismic thrusts along the fault.

Tomales Backroads

Millions of years ago, the grinding motion of the San Andreas Fault zone formed a rift valley, where the surface of the earth has literally pulled apart, between the steep Inverness Ridge to the west and the gentler hills to the east. The waters of the sea submerged this fifteen-mile-long depression and created Tomales Bay, which extends in a southeast direction from its mouth to the quaint community of Point Reyes Station.

Just where the word "Tomales" comes from is a mystery. Some think it's the Miwok word for "west." Others think the Spanish corrupted a Miwok word that meant "bay." Whatever the origin of the name, the first Spanish explorers—fooled by the narrow length of the bay—at first thought it was a river; one taste of the brackish water revealed the truth.

In addition to approaching Tomales Bay from the south, the bay can also be reached from the east by driving along the scenic Point Reyes–Petaluma Road that leads about a dozen miles from the town of Petaluma and U.S. 101. The road passes the Marin French Cheese Company, owned and operated by the same family for five generations. With handmade cheeses like the traditional Camembert and innovative peppercorn brie, and with spacious picnic grounds and a duck pond, the cheese factory is worth a stop. Or from Petaluma take Bodega Avenue to the Tomales-Petaluma Road, which leads to the picturesque town of Tomales, just inland from the north end of the bay.

The rural character of Tomales Bay and the surrounding countryside is no accident. Beginning in the 1960s, after the county government proposed a plan to build a freeway, an airport, and a community college that would support another fifty thousand

people, residents battled to save the remaining open spaces. They purchased land, formed a trust agency that paid ranchers not to subdivide their land, and passed zoning laws. The battle won, the scenic landscape surrounding Tomales Bay has remained gloriously undeveloped.

Along the San Andreas Fault

The San Andreas Fault, the sometimes wobbly border between the Pacific Plate to the west and the North American Plate to the east, runs below the surface of Tomales Bay. The mountainous ridges of western Marin County along the bay have been crumpled

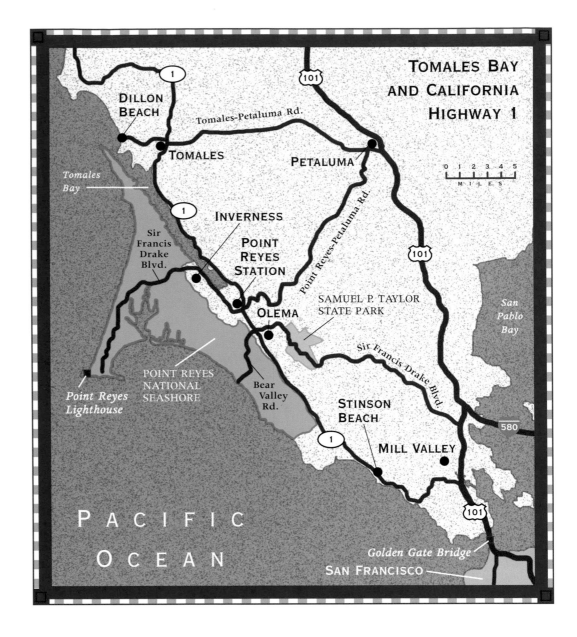

TOMALES BAY AND CALIFORNIA HIGHWAY 1

DILLON BEACH

Tomales-Petaluma Rd.

TOMALES

PETALUMA

Tomales Bay

INVERNESS

Sir Francis Drake Blvd.

POINT REYES STATION

Point Reyes-Petaluma Rd.

OLEMA

SAMUEL P. TAYLOR STATE PARK

San Pablo Bay

POINT REYES NATIONAL SEASHORE

Point Reyes Lighthouse

Bear Valley Rd.

Sir Francis Drake Blvd.

STINSON BEACH

MILL VALLEY

580

PACIFIC OCEAN

Golden Gate Bridge

SAN FRANCISCO

0 1 2 3 4 5 MILES

101

and pushed up by the movement of the earth below.

The epicenter of the great San Francisco Earthquake of April 18, 1906, was in the tiny town of Olema, just south of Point Reyes Station at the southern end of the bay. Fences across the fault line were broken and offset by seventeen feet. In fact, the entire Point Reyes Peninsula, on the west side of Tomales Bay, moved that distance to the northwest in an eye blink. By contrast, the steep, rolling hills on the peninsula normally slide north at a rate of about an inch per year.

To travel through the heart of earthquake country from the Bay Area, take U.S. 101

north from San Francisco. After crossing the Golden Gate Bridge, drive about fifteen miles to Mill Valley and take the Highway 1 exit. The highway winds up and over the slopes of Mount Tamalpais and drops down to the coast at Stinson Beach. From here, Highway 1 turns inland and continues about fifteen miles to reach tiny Olema. Bear Valley Road meets Highway 1 here, and leads northwest for a half mile to the Point Reyes National Seashore visitor center. Past the visitor center, Bear Valley Road ends at Sir Francis Drake Boulevard, which continues west through the little town of Inverness. With its late-nineteenth-century architecture,

TOMALES BAY, WITH THE NORTH AMERICAN PLATE ON THE RIGHT, THE PACIFIC PLATE ON THE LEFT, AND THE SAN ANDREAS FAULT RIGHT DOWN THE MIDDLE.

CALIFORNIA SKETCH: POCKET MARSHES

Tomales Bay is home to many animals, including harbor seals, Tule elk, and blacktailed deer. A great way to view the wildlife is by kayak, and there are at least a couple of places that rent kayaks along the bay. But a kayak is not required to take in much of what Tomales Bay has to offer. On my last visit to the bay, I watched from my car as half a dozen egrets hunted for crustaceans, fish, rodents, and other delicacies at the north end of the bay.

The egrets I saw were in one of several tiny saltwater marshes—biologists call them pocket marshes—which are the inadvertent aftermath of a nineteenth-century feat of engineering. The pocket marshes are behind a levee that was once the bed of the narrow-gauge railroad that carried tourists from San Francisco to the Russian River. The rail line also hauled local cheese and butter, oysters, fish, and Russian River redwood boards back to the city. The portion of the bay on the landward side of the levee, cut off from the main body of the water to the west, turned into little saltwater wetlands known as pocket marshes.

AN EGRET IN A POCKET MARSH ALONG THE NORTHERN END OF TOMALES BAY SEARCHES FOR A MEAL.

From Point Reyes Station, the train chugged north along the eastern edge of Tomales Bay, stopping at the towns of Bivalve, Millerton, Marconi (now a State Parks conference center), and Marshall, before turning inland and steaming further north to the river. Much of the levee is still visible, and so are the pocket marshes.

RIGHT:
A FARMSTEAD ALONG
SIR FRANCIS DRAKE
BOULEVARD, BETWEEN
OLEMA AND SAMUEL P.
TAYLOR STATE PARK.

FACING PAGE:
BACKLIT FERNS NEAR
SAMUEL P. TAYLOR
STATE PARK.

Inverness has managed to keep its charm while serving as a resort and seaport.

Inverness was founded in 1889 by James Shafter, a lawyer and ranch owner who had helped finance the narrow-gauge railroad that ran across Tomales Bay. To pay off his debt, Shafter subdivided 640 acres he owned on the shore of Tomales Bay and sold them to the new resort town of Inverness. Shafter reputedly named the town for his family's ancestral home, Inverness, Scotland.

Beyond Inverness, Sir Francis Drake Boulevard continues north through Point Reyes National Seashore. With 71,046 acres, Point Reyes National Seashore offers miles of trails for hiking, biking, and horseback riding. It's also a good place to watch for gray whales, which can be seen passing by California in December and January during their southern migration, and again in March through May during their northward migration from Mexico to Alaska. Point Reyes is also a good place to explore tide pools along rocky stretches of the coast, where it's not too difficult to find sea stars, sea urchins, and hermit crabs. The southern edge of the national seashore, Drake's Bay (where Sir Francis Drake probably first made land in Califor-

nia), and the Point Reyes Lighthouse, can also be explored.

If you follow Sir Francis Drake Boulevard in the opposite direction, it leads back to Highway 1. Traveling north, the highway continues along the east shore of Tomales Bay, past the levees and the pocket marshes and a few picturesque communities, including Point Reyes Station, with a main street just three blocks long, and from where the last train chugged off from Tomales Bay in 1933. The restored train depot is now the town post office.

Highway 1 turns away from Tomales Bay to reach the town of Tomales, which, with its one intersection, is even smaller than Point Reyes Station. Tomales, what there is of it, boasts a rustic architecture that is perhaps best described as "frontier Victorian." A road west of Tomales leads down through rolling pastureland to Dillon Beach, another resort town dating to the last century. Mostly a collection of beach houses, Dillon Beach also boasts Lawson's Resort, which offers vacation rentals and access to the beach. Lawson's Landing, another resort just to the north, has a fishing dock, boat rentals, and a campground.

On the ride down to Dillon Beach, it's easy to see where Tomales Bay opens to the sea. It's not so easy to comprehend the grinding force of nature that created the opening so long ago. That force ran on a slow timetable. But it was just as effective at creating Tomales Bay as the narrow-gauge railroad would be at creating pocket marshes millions of years down the line.

Samuel P. Taylor State Park

The exquisite Samuel P. Taylor State Park is in the coastal mountains about six miles southeast of Olema on Sir Francis Drake Boulevard. The park's campground is in a grove of redwoods, and several miles of hiking trails wind through the park's twenty-seven hundred acres.

Samuel P. Taylor purchased the future state parkland with money he made as a miner during the gold rush. He set up a sawmill, and in time, Taylor built a hotel that served guests from San Francisco. But a recession in the 1890s bankrupted Taylor. Adding insult to injury, the sawmill and hotel burned to the ground in 1916. Marin County took title to the land when the new owners couldn't pay the property tax, and the state created the park in 1946.

The campground is usually full during the summer, but when I pulled into the park one late April evening, the campground was almost deserted. I could just make out the towering trunks of the redwood trees by starlight, and I could hardly wait for morning to see them. I wasn't disappointed.

THE LOST COAST

Just the name, "The Lost Coast," should be enough to beckon a backroads aficionado. The rugged stretch of land, much of it wilderness, runs roughly one hundred miles from Eureka in the north to Rockport in the south. There are no major highways and only a sprinkling of small communities—heaven for the lover of backroads.

Ferndale

The northern portion of the Lost Coast can be explored on wild Mattole Road, which wanders for about sixty paved miles along the seacoast, up and down the coastal mountains, over windswept ridges, through meadows and pasturelands, and into Humboldt Redwoods State Park.

Mattole Road begins twenty miles south of Eureka in the Victorian village of Ferndale. To reach Ferndale from Eureka, take the Fernbridge/Ferndale exit from U.S. 101 onto California Highway 211. Cross the Eel River via the Fernbridge, which was the world's longest concrete arch span when it was built in 1911. Five miles farther down the road you will reach what many call the best-preserved Victorian village in America. The entire town of Ferndale is designated as a California Historical Landmark and is

THE 1898 NEW YORK CASH STORE IN THE VICTORIAN VILLAGE OF FERNDALE.

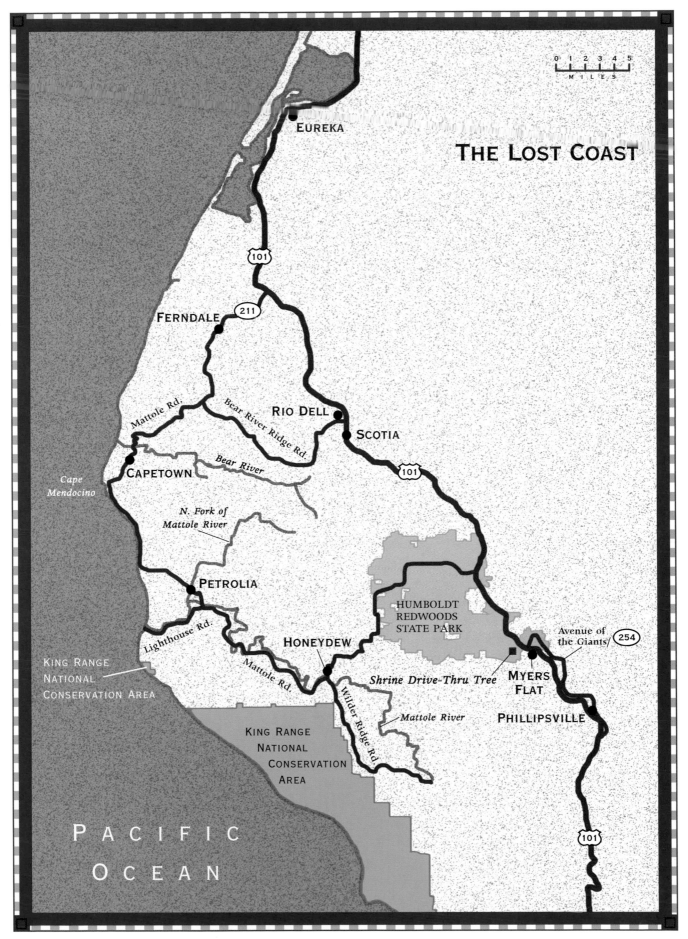

THE LOST COAST

0 1 2 3 4 5
MILES

EUREKA

101

211

FERNDALE

Mattole Rd.

Bear River Ridge Rd.

RIO DELL

SCOTIA

Bear River

CAPETOWN

101

*Cape
Mendocino*

*N. Fork of
Mattole River*

PETROLIA

HUMBOLDT
REDWOODS
STATE PARK

*Avenue of
the Giants/*

254

HONEYDEW

Lighthouse Rd.

Shrine Drive-Thru Tree

MYERS
FLAT

KING RANGE
NATIONAL
CONSERVATION AREA

Mattole Rd.

Wilder Ridge Rd.

Mattole River

PHILLIPSVILLE

KING RANGE
NATIONAL
CONSERVATION
AREA

P A C I F I C

O C E A N

101

on the National Register of Historic Places.

Ferndale was settled by two brothers, Seth and Stephen Shaw in 1852 when they began clearing land south of the Eel River. Seth built the first large house in 1854, naming his home Fern Dale. The house, considered a prime example of Carpenter-Gothic architecture, still stands on Main Street and is now known as the Shaw House. It is one of many Victorian mansions in the town that became Ferndale.

Scandinavians, Portuguese, and Swiss-Italians created a prosperous dairy industry that grew up around Ferndale in the late 1800s and supported the construction of the town's spectacular Victorian mansions, known as "Butterfat Palaces." With eleven creameries nearby, Ferndale was also known as Cream City. Today, there is only one creamery, but Ferndale is still surrounded by dairy farms.

Mattole Road

Mattole Road, named for the Mattole tribe that once inhabited the region, begins one long block west of Main Street and Ocean Avenue in Ferndale. At the start of the road, an iron sign with the town names "Capetown-Petrolia" sits atop two tall wooden poles. Originally the road was just a trail across cattle and sheep ranches over the coastal hills and mountains between Ferndale and the Bear and Mattole Valleys to the south.

Today, Mattole Road twists and turns and climbs for about five miles, first past sandstone cliffs that were once underwater, then through forests of Douglas fir. Along the way the road intersects with Bear River Ridge Road. This spectacular road follows a windswept, mostly treeless ridge overlooking the Bear River valley. Much of the way is over a good dirt road offering panoramic views as the road makes a series of switchbacks before meeting Monument Road and heading north to reach U.S. 101 and the little town of Rio Dell, just across the Eel River from the lumber town of Scotia.

Six miles past the Bear River Ridge Road

turnoff, the Mattole Road begins a descent to the Bear River and Capetown. There is no town at Capetown, only a few ranch buildings and a one-room schoolhouse in a state of disrepair.

Beyond Capetown, the road climbs again, crisscrossing ridges before descending to the sea just south of Cape Mendocino, the westernmost point in the contiguous United States. The ruins of the Cape Mendocino Lighthouse, not visible from the road, are commemorated by a roadside plaque on the beach near Ocean House, the only residence along ten miles of coastline. There is a small pullout in front of a locked gate just up the hill from the plaque. A half mile walk beyond the gate leads to the lighthouse, though visitors make the trip at their own risk.

After following the coast for several miles, Mattole Road turns inland a little north of the Mattole River. Cresting a ridge, there is a view into the Mattole Valley and the village of Petrolia. In 1864, the first oil wells in California were drilled nearby, giving Petrolia its name.

Originally, the first white settlers in the valley—after displacing the Mattole tribe—raised sheep, cattle, and hogs and built sawmills and gristmills. For a short time crude oil ruled the lives of the Mattole Valley residents, but the boom of 1864 soon played out and the people of the Mattole Valley went back to farming and ranching. Around the turn of the century, someone discovered that the bark of a locally abundant tree, the tanoak, could be used to cure leather. Unfortunately, the tanoak trees were cut down faster than they could be regrown, and the leather-curing industry in the Mattole Valley ceased to exist as the trees disappeared. More efficient methods for leather curing have since been found, and today tanoaks have returned to add their beauty to the Mattole Valley.

But the lesson that a sustainable resource must be nurtured was forgotten. After World War II, loggers moved into the Mattole Valley again, cutting down the redwoods and

ABOVE:
THE VIEW SOUTH FROM
CAPE MENDOCINO ON
MATTOLE ROAD ALONG
THE LOST COAST.

LEFT:
THE VIEW FROM BEAR
RIVER RIDGE ROAD
ABOVE THE MATTOLE
ROAD ON THE LOST
COAST.

Douglas firs. Ranchers began to subdivide the land and cut numerous roads for the new property owners. The subsequent erosion of the cleared lands, easily triggered by the region's abundant rainfall and steep terrain, poured tons of sediment into the Mattole River. Salmon runs that once numbered more than thirty thousand fish dropped to a few hundred by the 1970s, and, similarly, runs of steelhead trout dropped precipitously. Both fish are anadromous, which means they spend their adult lives in the ocean and return to the freshwater streams where they were hatched.

By 1980, the first citizen-led attempt to rebuild the stocks of steelhead and salmon in the Pacific Northwest was underway in the Mattole Valley. Each year, volunteers help hatch and raise up to fifty thousand salmon, but less than five hundred may return to the Mattole River. Restoration efforts continue today.

Lighthouse Road leads from Petrolia down to the beach. The sixty-thousand-acre King Range National Conservation Area lies to the south, with thirty miles of wilderness coast accessible only to hikers.

Past Petrolia, the road winds up through the river valley to the "town" of Honeydew, which, until 1970, operated up to eight sawmills. With the decline of the timber industry, the town of Honeydew, surrounded by dairy farms, dwindled to a few homes and ranches, and one general store.

To the east, Mattole Road begins to climb more steeply as it reaches toward Humboldt Redwoods State Park. Wilder Ridge Road takes off from Honeydew to the south, continuing along the Lost Coast on a route that is mostly dirt.

Late one autumn afternoon, a friend and I passed through Honeydew on our way to Humboldt Redwoods State Park and the Albee Creek campground. We stopped alongside the road to scavenge some apparently abandoned scraps of wood for the campfire we planned for that night. As we started to drive off with our booty, a pickup truck pulled in behind us. We stopped, and the driver approached our car.

"This is your wood, isn't it?" we guessed, correctly. We paid the unsmiling owner five dollars for the five pieces of wood we'd accidentally filched and continued up into the mountains to the state park. We arrived at the campground on the night before it closed for the season. No one was on duty, and the remaining stacks of campfire wood were available at no charge.

Avenue of the Giants

The following morning, my friend and I drove for five miles on a narrow road between the giant trees of the Rockefeller Forest. This stand is the largest remaining old-growth coastal redwood forest in the world. Efforts to preserve the redwoods began in earnest in 1921. A few years later, John D. Rockefeller donated $2 million, enough money to set aside ten thousand acres, the core of the future Humboldt Redwoods State Park. Today, the park includes more than fifty-one thousand acres of redwoods, as well as campgrounds and hiking trails.

U.S. 101 runs along the eastern side of the park, and heads north about forty-five miles back to Eureka. The scenic alternative, the Avenue of the Giants, parallels U.S. 101 and the Eel River for thirty-two miles. Now labeled California Highway 254, this is the old route of U.S. 101. A free tour brochure is available at either end of the Avenue, and at the state park visitor center about halfway along the Avenue. The route travels in and out of dense stands of redwood groves, where some of the trees reach to a height of more than three hundred feet; many of these giants have stood for two thousand years. The sunlight filters through the green canopy high overhead to softly illuminate the interior of the groves, like the interior of a medieval cathedral lit by stained glass.

Stop the car and step into the woods for at least a few minutes. Because the massive redwood forest absorbs sound, it's almost preternaturally quiet along the Avenue of the Giants. Even the adjacent Eel River runs silently, except when it threatens to overflow its banks.

A number of little towns that were once part of the local timber industry now cater to tourists along the highway, with cafés, stores, gift shops, and motels, inns, and resorts. At Myers Flat, near the southern end of Humboldt Redwoods State Park, there is the privately owned Shrine Drive-Thru Tree. Farther south in Phillipsville, there is the One Log House, a single redwood tree that has been carved into three rooms.

Of course, it's also possible to retrace Mattole Road to the village of Honeydew, where the southern reaches of the Lost Coast will beckon the backroads traveler.

REDWOODS JUT TOWARD THE SKY ALONG THE AVENUE OF THE GIANTS.

PART II

THE
KLAMATH MOUNTAINS

About 130 million years ago, the ancestral Sierra Nevada Mountains literally cracked in two. In a process not completely understood by geologists, the northern half of the mountains then slid sixty miles over the

face of the earth to become the Klamaths, coming to rest in their new home in the northwest corner of California.

It is known that the Klamaths are composed primarily of sedimentary rocks that were crushed and heated by pressure until they recrystallized into metamorphic rocks. Later, molten magma welled up inside the Klamaths, as well as the severed Sierras. Underground water in the two mountain ranges was heated by the magma. The water carried dissolved quartz that squeezed into the fractures of the recrystallized rocks. When it cooled, the quartz sometimes contained gold.

Usually very little gold can be found in the snow-white veins of quartz that snake through the mountains. But once the Klamaths began to erode, the gold was set free and was carried along in streams. Sometimes the gold settled in concentrations high enough to be profitably mined. Discovery of this placer gold in 1848 set off the gold rush, first in the Sierras, and soon after in the Klamaths.

The erosion that created streambeds also cut riverbeds into the mountains, forming the Trinity, Klamath, and Smith Rivers.

Along their lower stretches, these rivers have been designated wild and scenic by the state, which protects them from dams and further development along their banks. They are also among the last major rivers in California to see substantial numbers of salmon and steelhead run unimpeded upstream. The rivers divide the Klamaths into subregions, with the Siskiyou Mountains in the north, the Salmon and Scott Mountains in the center of the range, and the Trinity Mountains in the south.

Historians think that Peter Skene Ogden, a chief trader with the Hudson's Bay Company, was the first person to record a written name for the Klamaths, when he explored "Clammitt" country in 1826–27. In his expedition journal, Ogden may have unintentionally corrupted the word *clairmentis*, used by French-Canadian trappers to describe the region. According to one historian, this may be a derivation of a word used by French-Canadian fur trappers to describe mist-covered mountains. It is more likely a corruption of the word variously spelled *Clemmet* or *Tlamath* that the Klamath Indians used to call a lake in what is today the Umpqua National Forest in Oregon. The tribe called themselves the Eukshikni, or Auksni, "people of the lake."

Before their lives were disrupted by whites, Native American tribes, such as the Klamath, Hupa, Yurok, and Wintu lived in remote, self-sufficient communities along the flat river valleys. Ogden described the American Indians who lived along the lower reaches of the Klamath River as "most numerous and friendly." He had a less charitable opinion of the native tribes in general, though, noting earlier in his journal on February 13, 1827, "We all know Indians are treacherous, bloodthirsty. The sooner the exterminating system be introduced among them, the better."

Indeed, the Native Americans of the Klamath Mountains were almost exterminated, and their is no question that tribal life was changed forever. But there was neither a great influx of Canadians nor Americans into the remote Klamaths following the initial

explorations. The steep, heavily forested realms of the Klamaths were difficult for settlers to penetrate. The forests are nourished with up to 140 inches of rain a year in some places, hiding the mountains under a thick cover of Douglas fir, coastal redwoods, maples, and madrone. In many ways, the rugged wilderness of the Klamath Mountains provided a barrier to the heavy development going on in other parts of California. Even today, there are few paved roads and relatively few unpaved logging roads in the region. The remote nature of the mountains also helps explain the belief held by some that a humanlike creature, variously known as Bigfoot or Sasquatch, conceals itself in the thick forests of northwestern California. Whether or not a Bigfoot lurks in the woods, there are plenty of other wonders to discover in the Klamaths.

WEAVERVILLE AND THE TRINITY ALPS

Many people believe the Trinity Alps— where spires and ridges tower over steep, forested canyons, alpine lakes, and emerald meadows—are the crown jewels of the Klamath Mountains. The Trinity peaks, amongst the highest in the Klamath region, are white with abundant quartz during the spring, summer, and fall. The mountains are white in winter, too, when they're mantled in snow. Seen in sunlight or storm, from up close or afar, no one can doubt that the Trinities are among California's most spectacularly rugged mountains.

A Rainstorm over the Mountains

My visit to the heart of the Trinity Alps Wilderness was not going well, and I certainly couldn't see the white peaks. I arrived at the Big Flat Campground at the end of the Coffee Creek Road, in the middle of the night, during a rainstorm, without a tent. My only shelter was the confines of my small rental car.

It was difficult to sleep in the contorted positions required in such close quarters. I

A CLEARING STORM IN THE TRINITY ALPS WILDERNESS ON COFFEE CREEK ROAD NEAR THE BIG FLAT CAMPGROUND.

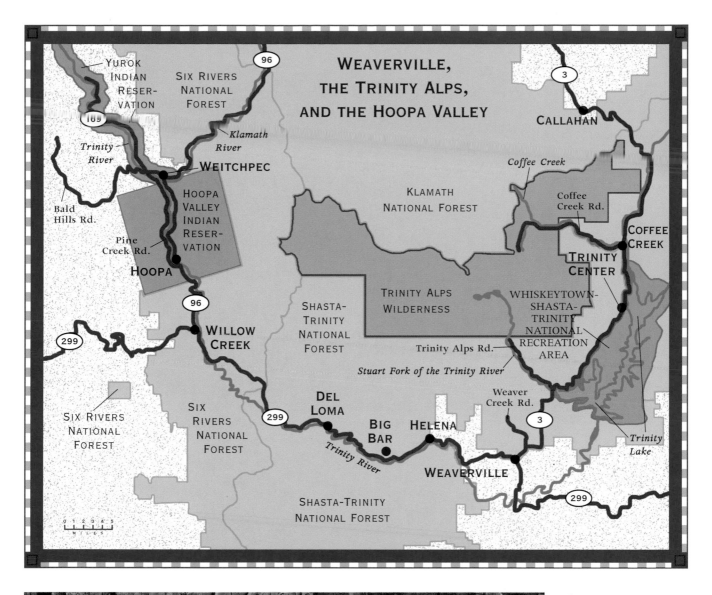

WEAVERVILLE,
THE TRINITY ALPS,
AND THE HOOPA VALLEY

YUROK INDIAN RESERVATION

SIX RIVERS NATIONAL FOREST

Klamath River

Trinity River

WEITCHPEC

Bald Hills Rd.

HOOPA VALLEY INDIAN RESERVATION

Pine Creek Rd.

HOOPA

SIX RIVERS NATIONAL FOREST

WILLOW CREEK

SHASTA-TRINITY NATIONAL FOREST

CALLAHAN

Coffee Creek

KLAMATH NATIONAL FOREST

Coffee Creek Rd.

COFFEE CREEK

TRINITY CENTER

TRINITY ALPS WILDERNESS

WHISKEYTOWN-SHASTA-TRINITY NATIONAL RECREATION AREA

Trinity Alps Rd.

Stuart Fork of the Trinity River

Weaver Creek Rd.

DEL LOMA

BIG BAR

HELENA

Trinity River

WEAVERVILLE

Trinity Lake

SHASTA-TRINITY NATIONAL FOREST

0 1 2 3 4 5 MILES

INSCRIPTIONS ON THE WEAVERVILLE JOSS HOUSE WALL LISTING GIFTS MADE TO THE TEMPLE BY ITS MEMBERS.

SPIRAL STAIRCASE, ONE OF THREE ALONG MAIN STREET; THIS ONE IS NEAR THE WEAVERVILLE DRUGSTORE, THE OLDEST IN CALIFORNIA.

Weaverville

In 1850, miner John Weaver and two friends drew straws for the honor of naming a little town that served as a supply depot for the gold rush. The town, at the base of the Trinity Alps, has been known as Weaverville ever since. With a convenient location at the junction of Highway 3 and Highway 299, Weaverville is a good place to begin exploring the country in and around the Trinity Alps.

Today, the economic base around the Trinity Alps rests on the timber industry and tourism. It wasn't so at the midpoint of the nineteenth century when Weaverville was the western locus of the California gold rush.

Gold was discovered in the Trinities in July 1848, at Reading's Bar on the Trinity River, only a few miles southeast of Weaverville. The discovery was made by Major Pierson B. Reading, a prominent Shasta County pioneer. Some people think Reading may have discovered gold as early as 1845, and, for whatever reason, kept quiet about it until the Sierra Nevada gold strikes of 1848.

The value of the gold mined in the Trinity Alps and surrounding Klamath Mountains was comparable to what was taken out of the Sierra Nevada foothills on the far side of the Central Valley. Strikes in and near Coffee Creek reputedly rivaled the Klondike finds in the Canadian Yukon a half century later.

During the height of the California gold rush, people from around the world lived in Weaverville. Thousands passed through on their way to the mining fields, their packs strapped to their backs or loaded onto mules as they made their way over rough mountain trails. Some miners arrived from the east, unloading their supplies from barges on the Sacramento River at Red Bluff, at the northern end of the Central Valley. Others traveled almost ninety mountainous miles from the West Coast, coming from the towns of Arcata and Blue Lake to establish claims

kept watching the sky in an agony of anticipation for signs that the storm was clearing. Just before dawn my suffering was rewarded. I awoke to see the full moon floating above the pines, glowing softly through a thin veil of clouds.

The Trinities are visible along California Highway 3 and California Highway 299. Foot and horse trails reach into 517,000 federally protected acres. Only Coffee Creek Road, a narrow corridor of private land penetrating deep into the heart of the Trinity Alps Wilderness, allows motorized travel into the wilderness, though the numerous backroads that skirt the edges of the wilderness provide spectacular views of the Alps and beyond.

on the creeks and cuts in the Trinity Mountains.

Several thousand Chinese—most from the province of Guangdong in southern China—arrived with the thousands of other gold miners, and by 1853 more than two thousand Chinese lived and worked in the Trinity Alps. Racially motivated incidents with white miners were not uncommon. Some of the racism was sanctioned by the government. For example, Chinese miners found themselves subject to a county "head tax" of four dollars per month. Caucasians were not subject to such a tax.

By the 1860s, when the surface gold had played out around the Trinity Alps, the Chinese left Weaverville, most of the men going to work on the transcontinental railroad under construction on the far side of the Sierra Nevada Mountains.

Weaverville's historic downtown district, rebuilt after fires in 1853 and 1854, contains several beautifully preserved brick buildings and three tightly spiraling, outdoor staircases along Main Street, which is also Highway 299. The Weaverville Drug Store, built in 1854, is the oldest such establishment in California; the courthouse dates back to 1856. The J. J. Jackson Museum and Historic Park offer another way to look at the history of Trinity County, with photographs, artifacts, and live demonstrations of the steam-powered Paymaster Stamp Mill, which crushed tons of rock pulled out of the mountains. The Weaverville Joss House is the oldest Chinese Taoist Temple in continuous use in California. Today the Joss House is also a museum and a state historic park.

Like the miners who passed through Weaverville so long ago, it's time for us to explore the Trinity Alps. We can begin by exploring the mountains that rise so abruptly to the northwest of the town.

Weaver Creek Road

The journey north from Weaverville to Coffee Creek begins in the middle of downtown, where Highway 3 meets Main Street. But about a mile north of town, where Highway 3 intersects with Weaver Creek Road on the left, a side trip beckons. This road passes through a residential area, where the deer like to nibble in private gardens, and then climbs up into the Trinity Mountains along Weaver Creek.

The paved road ends at a small national forest campground where Forest Service Road 34N34, leading into Shasta-Trinity National Forest, begins. This steep dirt road is sometimes impassable due to washouts. I had the logging road to myself one late evening as I headed past the campground. I drove along a ridge, high into the Trinities and far above Weaver Creek. After a good five miles I pulled off onto a flat spot in a clearing next to a pile of logs. I threw down my sleeping bag and elected to sleep under the stars and the half moon.

I awoke the next morning and stood atop the pile of logs, a little before the sun rose into an orange sky. Looking over the Trinities, I realized that Weaverville and any other sign or sound of civilization was absent. Except for the logging road, the scene looked as it may have looked to any Wintu Indian or mountain man who came before me.

California Highway 3

Retracing my route, I returned to Highway 3 and continued north onto national forest land. If it's a cool, early morning, this is a good stretch of road to watch for turkey vultures, who like to sit on tree branches and spread their wings to warm themselves in the slowly rising sun. At other times of the day, they can often be seen circling overhead, searching for carrion. They're easily recognized by their wobbly flight and large wingspan, which extends up to six feet. And, unlike eagles and hawks, the wingtips of a turkey vulture are spread apart, looking from a distance like fingers. Move in close enough and you'll see their featherless, red, turkeylike heads.

After a few more miles, Highway 3

reaches an arm of the massive Trinity Lake, part of the Whiskeytown-Shasta-Trinity National Recreation Area created by Congress in 1965. There is a good view here to the northwest of white granite peaks, rising over the lake

Just after reaching the lake, a side road — Trinity Alps Road—leads west along the Stuart Fork of the Trinity River. The road, mostly dirt, continues for three miles ending at the boundary of the Trinity Alps Wilderness where there is a campground and parking for the Stuart Fork Trail. The trail leads fifteen gentle miles up to Sapphire Lake. There is a nice view of the peaks and high ridges of the Trinities from the trailhead parking lot. From the lot, it's easy to see why the peaks were called the White Trinities.

Back on Highway 3, the road contours around Trinity Lake for a while. Trinity Lake, created by damming the Trinity River, began filling up the Trinity Valley in 1962. The area was once dotted with farms and ranches and towns established during the gold rush. The names of some of these submerged places—Minersville, Stringtown, the Scott Ranch—are only memories today.

The mountains beyond the end of the road were once called the White Trinities. They became known as the Trinity Alps after Mr. and Mrs. Anton Webber, who had traveled extensively in Europe, bought one of the old ranches and opened a resort on the Stuart Fork in 1922. The White Trinities reminded the Webbers of the Austrian Alps, and so they called their resort the Trinity Alps Resort. The name Trinity Alps caught on, and so it has been ever since.

From the shoreline of Trinity Lake, Highway 3 heads into a stretch of forest the Wintu called *Hunan Tsonos Loq,* translated as "Wolf Howls" (wolves once ranged this wilderness, though no howls have been heard anywhere in California for many years). The little resort community of Trinity Center is a few miles farther north. The town, serving miners and ranchers during the gold rush, was settled in 1851, and once had a population of twelve hundred people. Today there is a

DAWN ABOVE WEAVER CREEK, ALONG FOREST SERVICE ROAD 34N34 IN THE KLAMATH MOUNTAINS.

little country store and gas station, a marina and airport, homes, and the Sasquatch Restaurant, featuring a life-size statue of the famed, mythical monster.

This isn't the original site of Trinity Center. Sometime in the late 1850s the town was moved a few miles, evidently due to floods. One hundred years later the town moved again, this time to escape the rising waters of newly created Trinity Lake. Along with the people, several old buildings were moved to the new site.

Long before Trinity Center was founded, perhaps thousands of years ago, the Wintu settled here. They hunted deer and elk and collected acorns from the oaks. There were berries and seeds to gather in the summer, and salmon and steelhead to catch in the fall. The Wintu could take local sedges and willows and make them into baskets, woven so tightly that they held water without leaking.

Like most of the gold, the Wintu are gone from the Trinities. They died from the flu, from small pox, and from extermination at the hands of Caucasians. Despite their long occupation of the Trinity Valley, very little of their culture remains.

From Trinity Center, Highway 3 continues north along the Trinity Lake shoreline. Near the end of the lake, enormous mounds of bare rock and gravel come into view. These are mining tailings, testimony of gold-dredging operations around the turn of the century. As in the Sierra Nevada Mountains, the first miners in the Trinities had used shovels, picks, and pans to extract the gold from surface deposits. Then investors from the East Coast financed hydraulic mining operations that washed away entire mountains. The canyons and river valleys were next, where dredges removed the topsoil and left the piles of rocks and boulders that are visible today.

A FISHERMAN DRIFTS SILENTLY ACROSS TRINITY LAKE AN HOUR BEFORE SUNRISE.

About five miles past Trinity Center an older portion of Highway 3 runs a mile or so alongside horse pastures fringed with blackberry bushes, and past the impressive Carrville Inn, restored as a bed-and-breakfast. The inn was named by James E. Carr and his wife Sarah. James Carr was instrumental in building the California-Oregon Stage Road, which roughly follows Highway 3 today. At the beginning of the twentieth century, the inn served as a stagecoach stop, and Herbert Hoover, before he occupied the Oval Office, reportedly stayed there while working as a mining engineer.

Coffee Creek Road

Once back on Highway 3, it's another two miles to the little community of Coffee Creek. This is the northernmost outpost of civilization in Trinity County, the last community before the highway climbs over the Scott Mountain Divide into the Scott Valley and the town of Callahan.

From Coffee Creek, the Coffee Creek Road continues for nineteen convoluted miles up into the Trinity Alps Wilderness, offering spectacular views of forested slopes covered with pines, incense cedar, dogwood, oaks, and maples. Although the road is dirt, it's well graded and easily navigable by passenger car. Enormous piles of tailings fill the flatter portions of the canyon. These tailings, like those at Trinity Lake, also offer evidence of the mining activity that took place along Coffee Creek.

Gold rush miners named Coffee Creek, although how that name came to be is not precisely known. According to one story, a supply wagon loaded with coffee tipped over and poured its precious cargo into the creek. Another version claims the creek, normally clear, turns a rich coffee color during spring runoff when mud pours off the mountains.

The road levels out a bit as it nears the Big Flat Campground where Abram's Trading Post once stood, and where I spent that uncomfortable night in a rental car. James Abram built the trading post in 1850. He had searched for gold unsuccessfully the year before, and returned to build a stopover place for miners on their way from the Central Valley to diggings (mining excavation sites) along the Klamath River. Abram and his brother, who joined him a year later,

ABOVE, LEFT:
RESTAURANT IN TRINITY CENTER CELEBRATES THE LOCAL WILDLIFE.

ABOVE, RIGHT:
THE CARRVILLE INN, JUST OFF OF HIGHWAY 3, ONCE A HAVEN FOR TRAVELERS ON THE CALIFORNIA-OREGON STAGE ROAD, STILL OFFERS LUXURIOUS ACCOMMODATIONS FOR TODAY'S VISITORS.

built a store, a butcher shop, and a dairy building. The latter still stands and can be seen from the campground.

At Big Flat, near the headwaters of Coffee Creek, the public portion of the road ends at a locked gate, marking the entrance into Section 31 of the Shasta-Trinity National Forest. That one square mile of land behind the locked gate is privately owned, purchased by a California Supreme Court justice in the 1930s. While motorized travel is not allowed beyond the gate, except by the current landowners, any visitor has the right to hike on the road in order to reach the surrounding public lands.

There are some nice views of the mountains from the edge of the Big Flat Campground. However, it's worth walking about a mile farther, along reasonably level terrain, to view some of the spectacular high country peaks that lie beyond the locked gate.

The morning after the storm cleared (the night I spent camped in my car), I reveled in the sunlight as the mist slowly lifted off the Trinity Alps. Exploring along the road, I stopped to watch the clouds clear, and I met a couple who were burning piles of branches left over from timber cutting. I warmed myself around one of the fires for a few minutes on that damp, chilly autumn morning.

Thoroughly warmed, I decided to walk onto Section 31, hiking a mile or so through the woods to a meadow that offered a view of the White Trinities. Although the top of Josephine Peak, known locally as The Matterhorn, was still wreathed in a swirling mist, the clouds had lifted almost completely off the mountains and I could see that a light dusting of snow had fallen over the peaks during the night.

Time for my visit was growing short, so reluctantly I returned to my car and drove back down Coffee Creek Road.

THE HOOPA VALLEY

The Trinity River, beyond Weaverville and the Trinity Alps, flows toward the sea. But before flowing into the Pacific, the Trinity turns north at the community of Willow Creek. A little before reaching its junction with the Klamath River, the Trinity flows through the Hoopa Valley Indian Reservation.

Backroads to Hoopa

There are some who believe the center of the universe is in northwest California. The only way to know for sure is to drive twenty-two miles on California Highway 96, along the Trinity River and into the heart of the Klamath Mountains.

One autumn day I decided to do just that. I left Weaverville on Highway 299, following the westward flow of the Trinity River. Along the way I passed by Helena, a gold rush–era ghost town, as well as a few old-fashioned resort towns like Big Bar and Del Loma. At the latter, I perused a brochure at the Blue Cabins Motel describing the route along a steep trail leading to the Del Loma Cave. The brochure also said the cave extends for miles inside the Klamath Mountains. "To enter the cave," I read, "you must go down a rope 10 feet, down a 45 degree slide, then 15 feet on your back to a cliff, which is 20 feet high." I decided to visit the cave some other time.

After fifty-five miles I reached the little resort community of Willow Creek and the southern end of Highway 96 (Highway 299 continues about forty-five miles to unite with U.S. 101 near the town of Arcata). The intersection of the two highways is adorned with a statue of Bigfoot; the Willow Creek–China Flat Museum, just past the statue, provides information about the creature.

Much of Willow Creek was damaged in the great flood of 1964. A few of the buildings on the north side of town were washed across the highway to the south side. It was easier to rebuild them where they came to rest rather than drag them back across the road.

Hoopa

Highway 96 first travels north through farmland on the west side of the wide, flat Trin-

ABOVE:
THE GOLD RUSH—ERA
GHOST TOWN OF HELENA
SITS JUST OFF
HIGHWAY 299, ALONG
THE TRINITY RIVER.

RIGHT:
THE WEITCHPEC BRIDGE
SPANS THE KLAMATH
RIVER, JUST UPSTREAM
FROM ITS JUNCTION
WITH THE TRINITY
RIVER.

ity River valley. Four miles past Willow Creek I stopped at the Trinity River Farm produce stand, a local fixture. The owner, Tom O'Gorman, and his assistant, Lee Piola, were working the stand. The month was October, and harvest time was winding down. Even so, there were baskets full of colorful fruit and vegetables on display, and pumpkins ripened in a nearby field. I purchased some fruit for lunch, and Lee cut me a few slices of melon to sample.

For the next seven miles the highway climbs up the thickly forested mountain slopes overlooking the river, and the wide valley narrows into a canyon. There are Douglas firs here, as well as maples, madrones, and oaks. The road winds around a bend to reach the southern boundary of the Hoopa Valley Indian Reservation. The river canyon opens into the broad Hoopa Valley, surrounded by tall mountains that are often mantled with fog. The view is so lovely that it's easy to imagine this is indeed the center of the universe.

The Hupa (the people are known as the "Hupa," the reservation and valley are spelled "Hoopa") have always lived within the confines of the surrounding mountains, where the rhythms of life are observed with great care. During and after the gold rush, miners and settlers greatly disrupted those rhythms by trying to take the valley for themselves, either by forcing the Hupa off their land or by exterminating them. Because Hupa leaders like Captain John counseled accommodation where possible with outsiders, and because those willing to fight did so outside the valley, the Hupa were able to stave off large-scale violence in their homeland. Later, they were able to retain control of their land by signing treaties with the U.S. government, a government that was somewhat sympathetic to the plight of the Hupa.

The U.S. government established a reservation for the Hupa in the valley in 1864. Government officials believed the introduction of roads, schools, frame houses, modern clothing, and land titles would "civilize" their "primitive" charges; as a result, the government spent more than seven futile decades trying to suppress, disrupt, and destroy the traditional rhythms of Hupa life under the banner of civilization. Today, however, the Hupa still hold ceremonies like the White Deerskin Dance and still fish for salmon in the Trinity River as their ancestors did for thousands of years. After 150 years of strife, their destiny is now largely their own.

On my trip I stopped at a spot overlooking the ancient village of Tish Tang, where ceremonial sweat lodges have been reconstructed. Then I descended into the valley and drove past bucolic farms. A few miles later, I entered the little community of Hoopa in the center of the valley, a town known for its beautiful setting and powerhouse high school basketball team that regularly trounces all rivals.

Weitchpec and Beyond

A few miles past the village of Hoopa, the mountains close in again and the road climbs the east side of the canyon. The Klamath River, the northern boundary of the Hoopa Valley Indian Reservation, lies a few miles farther. The Trinity flows into the Klamath River here, and the impressive Weitchpec Bridge spans the Klamath a little above its junction with the Trinity. The graceful, twin arches of the bridge rise more than one hundred feet above the water. By the south end of the bridge, there is a little store that is a good place to get a cup of coffee or share a bit of conversation with the locals. The tiny community of Weitchpec, which is within the Yurok Indian Reservation, awaits on the opposite bank of the river.

If you travel west for 30 miles over mostly dirt roads, you will reach Redwood National Park. Highway 96 travels 130 miles northeast, upstream along the Klamath River, to the town of Yreka and on to Interstate 5.

But stay on the reservations for a while. Bring a good road map and search out the backroads and scenic spots in and around the valleys. On my trip, I drove up Big Hill Lookout Road, east of Hoopa, where I found stupendous views of the Hoopa Valley. I also traveled across the Weitchpec Bridge, and turned left onto California Highway 169. I drove three miles west, along the Klamath River, to Martins Ferry, the site of another river crossing on a big bridge. I crossed it to reach Tully Creek Road, and headed a quarter mile south to the intersection with Bald Hills Road and Pine Creek Road. To the right, Bald Hills Road leads another eighteen miles to Redwood National Park. But instead of traveling to the park, I veered left onto the unmarked Pine Creek Road, which leads back to Hoopa. Once the road reaches the Trinity River canyon, it winds its way above the west side of the river for eleven miles. Much of this road is dirt, and it does occasionally wash out in the winter, so it's a good idea to check locally to see if it's open. Don't expect to see any other vehicles, and be prepared to savor a leisurely ride through the forest, with occasional views of the river. The road climbs one last time before it comes around a bend to offer a spectacular, bird's-eye view of the Hoopa Valley and the encompassing Klamath Mountains.

PART III

THE

CENTRAL VALLEY

The Central Valley of California lies between the Sierra Nevada Mountains on the east and the Coast Ranges on the west. Other names, all appropriate, have occasionally been used for the valley, including the Great Valley, the Great Central Valley, and the Great Interior Valley. By whatever name, the Central Valley is enormous, stretching 450 miles in length and 50 miles in width through the heart of the state. Vermont and New Hampshire combined don't have as much real estate.

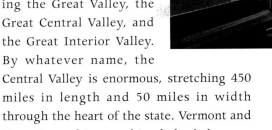

The Central Valley is known by separate names in its northern and southern halves. In the north, it is called the Sacramento Valley; in the south it's the San Joaquin Valley. The two names derive from the major river in each region. For the sake of consistency, we'll use the Central Valley designation in these pages.

Two major highways stretch the length of the vast valley. Interstate 5 is four to eight lanes wide and runs along the valley's west side, while the older California Highway 99 is on the east side. For the backroads aficionado, Highway 99 boasts only two lanes along portions of the roadway north of Sacramento.

But the best backroads in the Central Valley are the ones with more descriptive names, such as the Midway, Durham Ferry Road, and the Esplanade. These are the roads that travel right through the largest concentration of fruit farms, almond groves, and vineyards in the United States. These are the roads that travel to little towns and wildlife refuges never glimpsed from the main highways. And these are the roads that offer sweeping views of the foothills and mountains that define the very nature of the Central Valley.

The geologic record of the Central Valley stretches back perhaps 140 million years to the middle of the Cretaceous Period, when dinosaurs still walked over the earth and their aquatic cousins swam in its seas.

We will probably never know how the Central Valley formed, as the precise geological origins of the valley are buried in the thousands of feet of sediment that lie beneath the surface. However, we do know that similar valleys are found at the edges of continents, as well as in Japan, the Philippine Islands, and Alaska's Aleutian Islands. According to the best guess of geologists, the Central Valley probably began as an isolated arm of a western sea, separated from the main body of water by the crumpled rocks of the Coast Ranges, which first rose as a chain of islands. At the same time, the movement of the earth's crust pulled the Klamath Mountains apart from the northern

INSET:
SHUBERT'S ICE CREAM & CANDY SHOP IN CHICO ON A WARM SUMMER NIGHT.

FACING PAGE:
CHINESE PISTACHE TREES, PLANTED IN MEMORY OF THE MEMBERS OF THE DURHAM LADIES CLUB, LINE THE MIDWAY, THE OLD ROUTE OF HIGHWAY 99.

end of the Sierra Nevada Mountains. The Klamaths were ultimately offset from the Sierras by sixty miles, and today the Klamaths border the north end of the Central Valley.

Over the next several million years, the coastal mountains washed their muddy sediments onto the isolated sea floor. Sediments were also washed out of the Sierra Nevada, the Klamaths, and the Cascades. The inland sea was cut off from its source, and the invading sediments slowly settled to create the fertile Central Valley. Fifty million years ago the inland sea was already quite shallow. For the past 1.5 million years, most of the valley floor has rested little above sea level.

We know, too, that life permeated the primeval, inland sea before it filled with mud. The fossil record shows there were sea urchins, clams, fish, sharks, water birds, and marine reptiles. The mosasaurs were among the latter. The voracious mosasaurs, some more than thirty feet long, were predators at the top of the food chain. Adapted for aquatic life, the reptiles had limbs like hydrofoils and a large jaw filled with sharp teeth.

Once the sea dried up, somewhat less frightening forms of life moved into the valley. Mammoths roamed the valley floor more than a million years ago, and, about twenty thousand years ago, bison and now extinct species of giant ground sloths and horses grazed the plain—animals tantalizing to the humans that were soon to arrive.

The first humans settled in the Central Valley perhaps ten thousand years ago. Whenever they arrived, the earliest Californians found elk, deer, and pronghorn in profusion. They may have also hunted bison and horses. Archeologists have discovered that a flourishing culture, based on hunting and gathering, was in place by 2500 B.C., particularly on the west side of the Central Valley, in the Sacramento River Delta, and around San Francisco Bay. Where the culture came from, whether it developed eons earlier in California itself or in some other part of the North American continent, is not known.

The Spanish explored the Central Valley in the early eighteenth century, traveling first along the Sacramento River where they found Native American villages of the Miwok, Maidu, Wintu, Patwin, and Yokut. It is estimated that, at the time of the first Spanish settlement in 1769, over 76,000 American Indians lived in the north end of the Central Valley and almost 84,000 in the south, out of a total California population of 310,000.

The Spanish found several villages with more than a thousand inhabitants each, living in simple, earthen round houses. The Spanish also came across larger, ceremonial round houses, the most complex architectural structures built by California Indians. Dancers performed rites in these round houses to ensure the renewal of the earth each year. Today, two of these ceremonial round houses, in and near Yosemite National Park, are open to the public.

Jedediah Strong Smith was a mountain man and one of the first Americans to explore the Central Valley, first in 1827 and again the following year. Smith kept a journal, and a number of observations about the Native Americans he encountered are recorded in the fragments that survive. On his second journey, he reported that some American Indians "were under the impression that horses could understand them and when they were passing they talked to them and made signs to them as men." Far from appreciating the simplicity of the round houses, Smith described the method of construction as being "inferior to the Beaver," although he noted in his diary entry for March 21, 1828, that the Native Americans themselves were "honest and peaceable in their dispositions."

The pace of life in the Central Valley was little altered over the course of the first ninety-eight centuries of human habitation. But change accelerated with the coming of the Spanish, whose ranchos displaced the Native American communities. Later, Americans arrived in great numbers, and during the gold rush, towns sprang up to serve the mining camps in the Sierra Nevada foothills. Soon, railroads arrived to serve the towns.

Rough footpaths and horse trails have become crowded, four-lane highways and quiet, two-lane backroads. Wagons hauling the agricultural produce of the valley metamorphosed into trucks, trains, and even ships that navigate man-made channels to the sea.

Vast stands of oak and grasslands, once home to elk, deer, and grizzly bears, have been cut down. Now, country roads wind through fields of rice and corn, and groves of walnut and almond trees. Creatures large and small—on two legs and four, or who slither on the ground and fly overhead—can still be seen, often in the wildlife refuges found up and down the Central Valley.

Quaint towns that host weekly farmers' markets have sprouted throughout the valley. Where there were once simple Indian dwellings, today there are well-preserved and restored Victorian mansions to seek out, both in town and in the country.

The Central Valley has changed dramatically over the last two hundred years, but the sweeping views of the surrounding mountains look the same now as they did to the first Native Americans, Spanish, and Americans who arrived here. Indeed today's travelers have much to discover on their own along the backroads of the Central Valley.

MODESTO TO MANTECA

Our first tour lies within the southern confines of the Central Valley. The land here is drained by the San Joaquin River and sprinkled with a few big towns and numerous farming communities, which are linked by myriad backroads.

Modesto

It is possible to travel on the freeway less than twenty-five miles in an almost straight line between the quintessential Central Valley towns of Modesto and Manteca. But it is just as feasible, and a lot more fun, to take a more leisurely, decidedly circuitous tour that includes two rivers, two nature preserves, and a view of the San Joaquin Valley that predates its more recent agricultural heritage.

Our trip begins off Highway 99 in Modesto, a mid-sized town founded in 1870 as a railroad center on the banks of the Tuolumne River. According to local legend, the citizens of the town wanted to name it after the man chosen to be their first mayor, banker William C. Ralston, but he declined the offer. The citizens decided to honor his humility by calling the new town Modesto, the Spanish word for "modest."

West of Modesto

After exiting the freeway at California Highway 132, which is also Maze Boulevard, our route heads west, away from the city center. At first, the highway runs through the town's western business district and then past several blocks of neatly kept homes. Within a few miles, though, the scenery becomes unequivocally rural. Flat farmland filled with walnut and almond groves and occasional vineyards dominate the landscape. More distant views are possible on clear days; the mountains of the Coast Ranges are visible, beyond which lies the Bay Area, ninety miles away.

About ten miles west of Modesto, the San Joaquin River appears on the south side of the highway and parallels it for a short distance. The river veers abruptly back to the south and then just as abruptly returns to cross the highway under a bridge. At this point the San Joaquin River, now joined by the Tuolumne River, runs through the unmarked San Joaquin River National Wildlife Refuge. With eight hundred acres of riverside habitat, the refuge lies on either side of the highway, though there is currently no public access into the refuge. As the refuge is home to ducks, egrets, and sandhill cranes, and is the winter home to endangered Aleutian Canada geese, it's not a bad idea to keep one eye on the skies or the adjacent countryside.

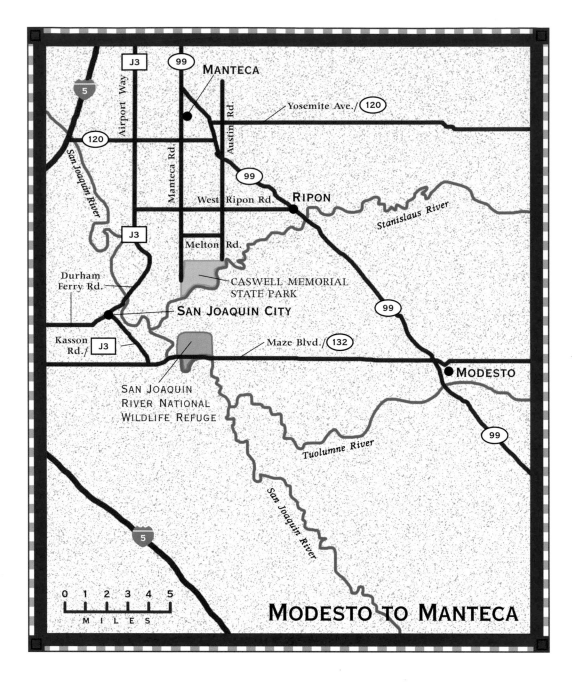

MODESTO TO MANTECA

San Joaquin City

Highway 132 reaches Kasson Road (County Road J3) a short distance past the bridge. Turn right and follow Kasson northward. The San Joaquin River, though not immediately visible from the road, meanders northward, too, toward the Sacramento River Delta. An old farmhouse, restored to its original 1908 splendor, stands on the east side of the road.

San Joaquin City, its existence noted only by a road marker along Kasson Road, was a thriving river town in 1849. Impor-

tant in the development of farming and ranching on the west side of the Central Valley, San Joaquin City was a terminus for riverboats plying the San Joaquin River.

At San Joaquin City, Kasson Road reaches the intersection with Durham Ferry Road, which County Road J3 now follows, and where a little country store serves the local population. Turning right, you will again cross over the San Joaquin River. Soon, Durham Ferry Road becomes Airport Way, which swings away from the river and then continues on a straight line past walnut groves, cornfields, and vineyards. Airport Way eventually reaches the west side of Manteca and, then, Stockton.

Caswell Memorial State Park

Our tour, however, turns right a few miles shy of Manteca onto West Ripon Road. For about five miles the road doubles back toward Highway 99 and the little town of Ripon. But before reaching Highway 99, turn right onto Austin Road, which dead-ends a few miles later at Caswell Memorial State Park.

This small nature preserve safeguards one of the last riverside woodlands in the San Joaquin Valley. The park is worth more than a cursory visit and the entry fee is nominal. The Stanislaus River meanders past trails, beaches, picnic areas, and a campground with many secluded sites. Catfish, bullhead, buffalo carp, and several other species of fish swim in the cool river waters, which flow into the nearby San Joaquin River.

At Caswell there is, as naturalist John Muir wrote about these riverside woodlands, "a fine jungle of tropical luxuriance, composed of wild-rose and bramble bushes and a great variety of climbing vines, wreathing and interlacing the branches and trunks of willows and alders." Like a tropical forest, the trees at Caswell have created a canopy of leaves that, during the summer, can keep temperatures inside the park ten degrees cooler than the surrounding San Joaquin Valley.

During the summer, too, the leaves of wild grapevines completely (and harmlessly) cover even the tallest valley oaks, which are the largest species of oak in the United States. Some of the trees in the park are more than sixty feet high.

My favorite time to be in the park is early morning. Sunlight makes its way down from the tops of the trees in an often futile effort to penetrate the interior of the woods. This is the time to look for great blue herons lounging along the river, and to watch out for spiders and their webs that stretch alongside and across the several miles of trails that wind through the oaks. I've watched ringtails and foxes plunge into the underbrush at my approach; raccoons, skunks, and opossums are also common here. Two extremely rare animals, the riparian brush rabbit and the riparian woodrat, also inhabit these forests and are protected in the park.

Dusk, too, is a lovely time to be at Caswell, as the setting sun throws a golden light over the trees, and the sounds of crickets and frogs presage the coming of night.

In California, most of the riparian (or riverside) woodlands have been decimated by flood control projects and the clearing of land for agriculture. Before the mid-1800s,

THE STANISLAUS RIVER AT SUNSET IN CASWELL MEMORIAL STATE PARK.

ABOVE, TOP:
SUNSET OVER THE
CENTRAL VALLEY, FROM
AUSTIN ROAD LOOKING
WEST ALONG MELTON
ROAD, NEAR CASWELL
MEMORIAL STATE PARK.

ABOVE, BOTTOM:
COLORFUL WHEELS AND
GARDENS ADORN A
FARM NEAR MANTECA IN
THE CENTRAL VALLEY.

While hiking through the park, you may find a plaque, which tells a story about the man who gave the Stanislaus River its name. In 1829 an apostate American Indian, Estanislao, led a band of followers against Mexican soldiers near what is today the Stanislaus River. Until American occupation almost two decades later, the river was called Rio de Estanislao. Today, the river's English name still honors the Native American chieftain.

When it's time to leave Caswell Memorial State Park, return via Austin Road. Melton Road, the first left as you follow Austin Road north, offers a shortcut to Manteca Road, which in turn leads directly north into the town of Manteca. The road crosses over California Highway 120, which is a four-lane freeway that bypasses Manteca just south of the town.

Manteca

Manteca bills itself as the San Joaquin Valley entry to Yosemite. The old Highway 120, which ran through the center of town, is still named Yosemite Avenue. There is an obvious civic pride and historic charm to Manteca, evidenced in the renovation of its downtown streets and buildings.

The town was founded in 1861, not by railroad barons as in Modesto, but by a farmer, Joshua Cowell; Manteca was at first known as Cowell Station. In 1873, the Central Pacific Railroad laid tracks into Cowell Station. Because another Cowell Station, named after Joshua's brother, Wright, was located in nearby Tracy, the railroad and local farmers decided on a name change.

The new, local spelling of the town was *Monteca*, supposedly an archaic Spanish word for "butter." The word may have been chosen because a creamery stood near the first train station. When the passenger tickets were printed, however, *Monteca* was misspelled as "*Manteca*," which was, and is, the Spanish word for "lard."

Despite some local protest, the new name stuck and, in a way, Manteca's name turned out to be as modest as Modesto's.

much of the San Joaquin Valley's riverbanks and floodplains were covered with hardwood forests. Now, these woodlands are among the state's rarest ecosystems.

The land, which today is the park, came into the hands of Thomas Caswell in 1915. Mr. Caswell and his family farmed the land, but preserved the woodlands along the river. In 1950, Caswell's children and grandchildren donated 134 acres to the state. Later purchases by the state and local organizations created 258 acres of parkland.

It's possible to spend much of a day wandering over the park's trails. For those pressed for time, there are a few, short loop trails leading from two picnic areas that take hikers into the woods and alongside the river.

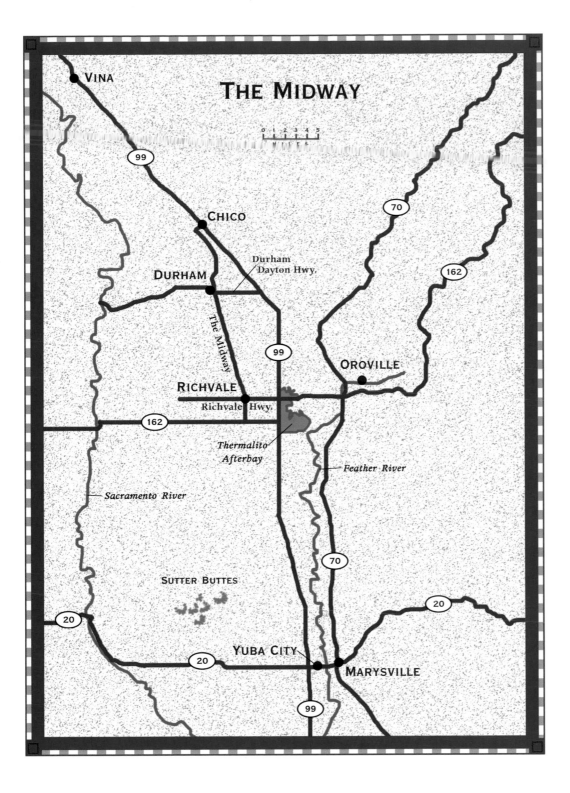

THE MIDWAY

The quickest, shortest way to reach Red Bluff from Sacramento is via Interstate 5. A more satisfying route follows old highways and country backroads that run between the Sacramento River to the west, and the Sierra Nevada and Cascade Mountains to the east.

Old Highway 99

I hadn't driven along the Midway—a two-lane stretch of road that runs from just to the south of the town of Richvale to Chico—since 1970. The Midway, reputedly the oldest concrete roadway in California, was once part of Highway 99, the Central Valley's first major roadway. Until the 1960s, when freeway bypasses were constructed, Highway 99 ran through the center of several towns.

In the early 1960s, the Highway 99 road-bed was rerouted about a mile east of the Midway, gaining two lanes and becoming a freeway. The Midway, no longer a state high-way, was relegated to the simple task of serv-ing local traffic. I had taken the old road a few times when I was a student at Cal State Chico, because I prided myself on explor-ing every backroad around Chico.

I had only vague memories of what the Midway looked like when I made my return trip one recent autumn. The Midway's chief attraction, I knew, was that it would take me off the busy Highway 99 freeway. I had driven north from Sacramento that morning through eighty miles of rice fields, as well as almond and walnut groves, ultimately on my way to destinations well north of Durham and Chico. About thirty miles north of Sacramento I passed the twin towns of Yuba City and Marysville, separated only by the Feather River. To the west I could see the striking Sutter Buttes, reputedly the world's smallest mountain chain. I crossed from Sutter County into Butte County and, still about nineteen miles from Chico, reached the junction of Highway 99 and California Highway 162.

If I had turned right, Highway 162 would have taken me east, into the city of Oroville, which sits up against the Sierra Nevada foothills. Instead, I turned left, heading west through a vast expanse of rice fields. Huge rice elevators and silos were visible in the distance. Highway 162, followed far enough west, winds up into the Coast Ranges, but today I drove only the first three miles along the highway and continued straight on the Richvale Highway when Highway 162 veered south.

I crossed a set of train tracks, and just beyond, I turned right onto the Midway. There were more rice fields along both sides of the narrow road. I passed through the little community of Richvale, where the most prominent structures were squat, round tanks where rice is first dried, and the adja-cent, tall rice silos that store rice before it's shipped by rail to Sacramento.

The tanks and silos belong to Lundberg Family Farms. The Lundbergs pioneered the production of pesticide-free rice in north-ern California in 1969. If you stop by the Lundberg headquarters in Richvale, you can ask for the recipe for brown rice waffles.

Continuing toward Durham, my view east was cut off by the slightly elevated road-bed of the train tracks which now paralleled the Midway. An egret stood on the west of side of the road, its feathers a bright white against the autumn-brown rice grass.

Durham

About ten miles past Richvale I arrived at the community of Durham. At the intersec-tion of the Midway and the Durham Dayton Highway, which makes up the center of the commercial district in town, I had a good cup of coffee at the French Bakery, across the road from the town's country store.

Durham suffered a disastrous fire in 1938, when a number of buildings, includ-ing all those dating to the gold rush, were destroyed. But the town can boast about its Durham House, a Victorian mansion, built in 1874 by William Durham for his bride, Minnie. The privately owned mansion, re-cently restored, is just east of the railroad tracks on the Durham Dayton Highway, and so escaped the conflagration that engulfed the center of town. In 1871, the California and Oregon Railroad laid tracks to a flour mill built by Durham, and "Durham's Stop" soon grew to become the community of Durham.

Durham to Chico

As I continued my drive north toward Chico, I marveled at the beautiful trees that lined each side of the Midway—trees I couldn't identify. There was a hint of the autumn color to come, with some of the elongated leaves showing pale red and orange. I parked at Hodge's Nursery, about a quarter of a mile

past the four-way stop sign in Durham. The owner, Ken Hodge, graciously showed me around his property and told me a little about those trees.

They were, Mr. Hodge explained, Chinese pistache trees, and he confirmed my suspicions that they would be ablaze with color in a few weeks. They were planted to honor the memory of various members of the Durham Ladies Club. "But the color won't last long," Mr. Hodge told me. "One good storm and the leaves will be gone." I told Mr. Hodge I would call in a few weeks to see if the trees were at their autumn best, so that I could photograph them (and have an excuse to return to the Midway). We said goodbye and I continued to the end of the Midway, crossing over the train tracks on a bridge leading into Chico.

Chico

The Midway changes names in Chico, becoming Park Avenue and then Main Street, but it is still the route of old Highway 99. Downtown Chico, complete with stoplights, is hardly a byway, but it has managed to

AUDREY BROCHHEUSER ON THE FRONT PORCH OF THE DURHAM HOUSE, HER HISTORIC HOME IN DURHAM.

CALIFORNIA SKETCH: THE BIDWELLS

John and Annie Bidwell were pioneers of both the physical and intellectual world, and it is no exaggeration to describe them as northern California's first Renaissance couple.

John Bidwell was born in New York in 1819. At the age of twenty-two, he lead the first group of settlers to reach California by an overland route. Bidwell's party consisted of about fifty-five men, women, and children. They crossed the plains with their wagons, but abandoned them in western Nevada so they could cross the Sierra Nevada, either at Sonora Pass, the route of what is now California Highway 108, or more likely at Ebbetts Pass, along present day State California Highway 4.

The discovery of gold on John Sutter's property would ignite the gold rush and secure Sutter's place in history. But before that momentous event, Bidwell became Sutter's protégé, serving as his general manager. Like Sutter before him, Bidwell received an extensive land grant from the Mexican government, which then controlled California. During the Mexican War (1846–1848), Bidwell served, perhaps more reluctantly than he wished to publicly admit, under John Fremont, the self-aggrandizing, controversial explorer, soldier, and political leader. After the war, Bidwell returned to his property in the Sacramento Valley. Like everyone else, he caught gold rush fever in 1848. Not a wealthy man, Bidwell mined along the Feather River, above present day Oroville, and struck it rich.

Bidwell subsequently purchased land along Chico Creek, in the upper end of the Sacramento Valley, where he built Bidwell Mansion, created an agricultural empire at Rancho Chico, served in the state senate and U.S. Congress, and ran unsuccessfully for both governor of California and the presidency of the United States.

Annie Ellicott Kennedy, the woman who would become John Bidwell's wife, met her future husband in 1865 while John was serving in Congress. The daughter of a socially prominent Washington official, Annie was devoutly pious and interested in the temperance and women's suffragist movements. Initially reluctant to leave Washington and the causes she believed in, Annie was eventually won over by the tall, handsome Bidwell, presumably swayed in part by the stream of letters Bidwell sent her after he retired from Congress and returned to California. They were married in 1868 in a Washington wedding attended by President Andrew Johnson and General Ulysses S. Grant.

John and Annie settled into Bidwell Mansion and engaged themselves with Rancho Chico. They also traveled extensively in Europe and along the east coast of the United

States. John joined Annie in championing womens' rights, and, although John Bidwell was renowned as a vintner before his marriage, his second run for the governorship of California and his symbolic try for the presidency were made as a temperance candidate. John and Annie were also interested in natural history, and they spent part of each summer camped in the Sierra Nevada or the Cascades, often joined by eminent naturalists and scientists.

The Bidwells were not controversial figures while they were alive. But their relationship with the Maidu has come under scrutiny, both by the descendants of the Maidu and by historians. During the gold rush, John Bidwell gave protection to the Maidu, allowing them to live on their ancestral lands within the confines of Bidwell's land grant. He also gave them work. At the time, most other Native Americans in California faced extermination or were forcibly removed to reservations.

Annie Bidwell became intimately concerned with the welfare of the Maidu. However, it would not be an exaggeration to say the Bidwells, particularly Annie, were paternalistic toward their charges. Annie Bidwell became a Presbyterian minister, performing marriages and baptisms for the Maidu. She taught them English, exchanged the Maidu's domed dwellings for houses, substituted sewing for basketry, and replaced the native cultural traditions and religious practices with western customs and Christian teachings.

Childless, Annie Bidwell called the Maidu "my children," and apparently did not mind being called "Mother Bidwell" by the Maidu. She may have been the stepmother to her husband's children, for John Bidwell supposedly had a physical relationship with at least one Maidu woman some years before Annie's arrival in Chico.

If Annie Bidwell knew about or even suspected her husband's earlier liaisons, then we can only conjecture what the implications might have been for the Bidwells and the Maidu. We do know that John Bidwell had written Annie, during his courtship, "Still I have thousands of faults which will often call for forgiveness on your part." He also wrote, "I want to live for you and the good we can do." On balance, it would seem the good that Annie and John Bidwell accomplished for themselves, for Chico, and for California far outweighs any of their faults.

ABOVE:

GENERAL JOHN AND MRS. ANNIE BIDWELL, CIRCA 1895. (COURTESY OF JOHN NOPLE.)

keep its small-town flavor and is far more fun to drive through than the freeway, just to the east.

Shubert's Ice Cream & Candy, on East Seventh Street, has been in operation since 1938, and has been owned and operated for four generations by the same family. I can remember enjoying an ice cream cone at Shubert's with my girlfriend on warm, summer evenings in the early 1970s. If you have a dog, the owners, Chuck and Kay Pullian, or their children, might treat your pet to some ice cream, too.

I noted one change from my own days in Chico: There are now a lot more bike shops. That wasn't a surprise, because Chico has since been voted the most "bike friendly" town in the nation. On a whim, I decided to stop at Pullins Cyclery, one of the town's bike shops that was there when I lived in Chico. I'd chatted a few times with old Mr. Pullin, whose shop was cluttered with old bike parts. The current owner, Steve O'Bryan, worked for Mr. Pullin as a high school student at the same time I was a student at Chico State.

Mr. O'Bryan enjoys repairing old bikes and telling a good story, thereby keeping alive two traditions that were long associated with his mentor. His shop boasted many of the most technologically sophisticated mountain bikes, but he was most proud of a restored Schwinn Deluxe Tornado.

After saying goodbye to Mr. O'Bryan I continued up Main Street, which becomes the Esplanade at the north end of downtown. Like the Midway, the Esplanade is lined with trees, though not the Chinese pistache. Instead, there were elms, flaming amber (sweetgum), and, along the center divider, ginkgo trees. Unlike the rural Midway, the Esplanade is also lined by a number of lovely homes, some dating from the last century.

The Bidwell Mansion sits just west of the Esplanade next to the beautiful Cal State Chico campus (also called Chico State). The mansion was built by the town's founder,

John Bidwell, and features a pink-tinted stucco exterior.

Construction for the mansion began in 1865 and lasted three years. Bidwell apparently wanted the mansion, which has twenty-six rooms, to look like an Italian villa. The college eventually took control of the mansion after the death of Bidwell's widow, Annie, using it at various times as a girls dormitory and a dining hall, as well as for classrooms and college dances. In 1964, California turned the mansion into a state historic park.

After visiting the mansion, I walked

PULLINS CYCLERY IN CHICO. THE CENTRAL VALLEY COLLEGE TOWN HAS BEEN VOTED THE MOST BIKE FRIENDLY TOWN IN THE COUNTRY.

across a footbridge spanning Big Chico Creek, which spills out of the mountains to make its way through the Chico State campus. Originally built on eight acres of a cherry orchard set aside by the Bidwells, the college was first named the Northern Branch of the State Normal School. It underwent a few other name changes—State Teachers College in 1921, Chico State in 1935, and California State University, Chico, in 1972. But for most people, including me, it's always going to be Chico Sate.

I walked past ivy-covered, red brick buildings, several of them featuring the classic collegiate look of Romanesque architecture with its domes, towers, and vaulted arches. There were flower and sculpture gardens, spacious lawns, and picnic tables along the tree-lined creek. I'd forgotten over the years I'd been away just how pretty the campus is.

Leaving the campus, I drove south through town, exploring streets near the college that boast a number of Victorian homes, including the majestic Stansbury Home at Fifth Street and Salem.

I rejoined Highway 99, which runs north of Chico for about forty miles on just two lanes of blacktop and ends at Red Bluff,

where the old highway joins busy Interstate 5. Along the way I stopped for a soft drink at the country store in the little community of Vina. I also spent some time here visiting the Abbey of New Clairvaux, a Roman Catholic monastery of the Trappist-Cistercian Order.

I sat on a stone bench and enjoyed the view of the farmlands worked by the monks, who earn their income by tending to French plum-prune trees, English Hartley and Vina walnut trees, and one hundred acres of grain. The land, once owned by pioneer Peter Lassen and then by the railroad magnate Leland Stanford, became a monastery in 1955. Stanford's grand mansion burned in 1972 and was not rebuilt.

I spoke with some of the monks, but they were generally not talkative. Although they do not take a vow of silence, they believe silent meditation is a fundamental requisite for living at New Clairvaux. They live communally in attached living quarters—cloisters—and have few material needs.

Visitors can stay in guest rooms, and while the monastery accepts contributions, there is no charge. Those who do stay are invited to join in the daily prayers, which begin at 3:30 A.M. After a day of work and meditation, the monks follow their final invocation, at 7:35 P.M., with what they call the Grand Silence, their well-deserved time of rest that lasts until early the following morning.

Autumn along the Midway

After I returned home, I didn't forget about those Chinese pistache trees. In late October, a few weeks after my trip up the Midway, I called Mr. Hodge in Durham to inquire about the fall color. "You'd better come soon," Mr. Hodge said. A day later, I said goodbye to my wife, dropped my youngest daughter off at school, and hit the road for Chico. It was well after dark when I arrived, so the colorful secrets of the Midway were hidden from me.

The next morning I drove a few minutes from a friend's home where I'd spent the night, to the Midway, which was alive with color. The low angle of the sun this late autumn morning made the long, translucent red and orange leaves of the Chinese pistache

trees appear as if they were lit by an interior light. Tall and broad, the trees not only lined the Midway, they arched over the road creating a canopy perhaps thirty feet high. There were walnut trees, too, growing in turn on the west side of the old highway—their leaves a golden color. I stopped at Hodge's Nursery again, and walked across the road to photograph a particularly colorful Chinese pistache, not just red, but crimson. After enjoying a cup of coffee in town, it was time to head for home.

Today, travelers are afforded no views of Durham or the Midway from Highway 99. Nor does the freeway offer a view of Bidwell Mansion, the Esplanade, or the college campus in Chico. Given the amount of traffic on Highway 99, Durham and Chico would be clogged with cars if the freeway hadn't been built. But those speeding by will miss a cup of coffee in a country store, a walk in the park, a good story, and towns enfolded in the colors of autumn.

A STONE BENCH BENEATH AN OAK TREE INVITES A MEDITATIVE MOMENT AT THE ABBEY OF NEW CLAIRVAUX IN VINA.

PART IV

THE DELTA: WHERE IT'S ALWAYS YESTERDAY

Time seems suspended in the Delta. Years ago, paddle-wheeled steamboats once put in at many little towns along the Sacramento River. The steamboats are gone, but the towns remain, some looking much as they did when they were built in the middle of the nineteenth century. The quiet Delta maintains its yesteryear feel— it is a pleasant place of picturesque towns, meandering waterways, islands of all shapes and sizes, and many backroads.

The Delta sits at the western edge of the Central Valley, east of the Bay Area and south of Sacramento. The Delta's 738,000 acres are home to rivers, sloughs, and deepwater channels. More than one thousand miles of levees protect fifty-five islands from flooding. Like a colossal magnet, the Delta pulls the sea on one side and two great rivers on the other, the Sacramento and the San Joaquin. The rivers unite in the Delta, pass through Carquinez Strait, and enter San Francisco Bay ultimately to flow into the Pacific Ocean beneath the Golden Gate Bridge.

The Delta is a popular destination for people who enjoy fishing, boating, and windsurfing. It's also a major habitat for migrating waterfowl. And its gentle, afternoon breezes tame the ferocious summer heat in nearby Sacramento.

Perhaps some thirty thousand Native Americans lived in the Delta before the arrival of Europeans. Spanish explorers Pedro Fages, who was also the military governor of Upper California, and Father Juan Crespi, a Franciscan missionary, were probably the first non-Indians to see the Delta. In March 1772, they viewed it from Mount Diablo, to the east of Oakland. At the time, the Delta rivers had overflowed their banks with spring runoff, and Fages noted in his journal that he thought he was looking at a vast inland sea.

Though Fages could not imagine it then, the ancient, uninterrupted cycle of flooding in the Delta would continue for less than 150 years. The cycle began to change with the discovery of gold at Sutter's Mill in 1848, which provided the impetus for the greatest gold rush in history, and brought an influx of people from around the world. After the gold played out, the people who stayed in California sought other ways to make their fortunes, and some of them turned their attention to the vast, unclaimed tidal marsh that was the Delta.

The federal government deeded the Delta to the new state of California in 1850, which in turn sold the land to developers. By 1871, the Delta was completely in private hands.

INSET:
A FIGURINE DECORATES A SHOP WINDOW ALONG MAIN STREET IN LOCKE.

FACING PAGE:
KAWAMURA BARBER SHOP ALONG THE MAIN STREET IN WALNUT GROVE. THE TOWN IS THE ONLY ONE IN THE DELTA THAT SITS ON BOTH SIDES OF THE SACRAMENTO RIVER.

The proceeds reaped by the state were used to build levees and pump dry the fertile peat soil of the region. Chinese laborers were paid thirteen cents for each cubic yard of soil they added to the first Delta levees, which were constructed to protect two islands, Twitchell and Sherman.

In the late 1870s, steam-powered "clamshell" dredges used giant teeth to move a cubic yard of soil for a cost of just five cents from the river channels to the levees. After 1918, nearly all Delta marshland had been drained, and the salt grass was replaced by cornfields and pear orchards. The last major change in the Delta took place in 1963 when a deepwater channel was completed, allowing cargo ships to bypass drawbridges that still dot the rest of the Delta.

Despite the dramatic changes in the land,

THE SUN RISES OVER THE SACRAMENTO RIVER IN THE DELTA.

the little towns along the Sacramento have remained much the same. The very nature of the enormous Delta, with its innumerable waterways and ever-present threat of flooding have kept the towns safe from unlimited development, or much development at all. The Delta, then, is one of those rare places where the past is palpable, where the need for nostalgia does not exist.

LOCKE AND THE DELTA

Perhaps no place in the Delta captures the region's relaxed (even sleepy) atmosphere, as well as its quirky sense of frozen time and space, like the town of Locke.

California Highway 12

One early summer afternoon my wife, Kathy, and I were on our way to Sacramento and a northern California vacation when we decided to make a leisurely detour through the Delta. A few miles past the Stockton city limits we exited Interstate 5 at its junction with Highway 12 and headed west.

The road ran straight for about five miles. We drove over the Terminous Bridge and entered Bouldin Island, which has a maximum elevation of about ten feet above sea level. Much of the landscape was covered with cornfields, and it was difficult for us to tell we were on an island.

Our pleasant journey across Bouldin Island was far different than the experience of James Corwin, who, in the summer of 1883, labored near here helping dredge the Delta to construct levees. As he wrote, "The weather is very hot, the water could not be worse no matter where it comes from, as it is muddy and green colors and filled with malaria, but we have to drink it for we can get none other. . . . The mosquitoes are terrible. When night comes they swarm around by the millions. . . ."

From Bouldin we crossed the Mokelumne River onto Andrus Island, and about a quarter mile later we turned right off of Highway 12 onto Terminous Road, providing a shortcut to Locke through the town of

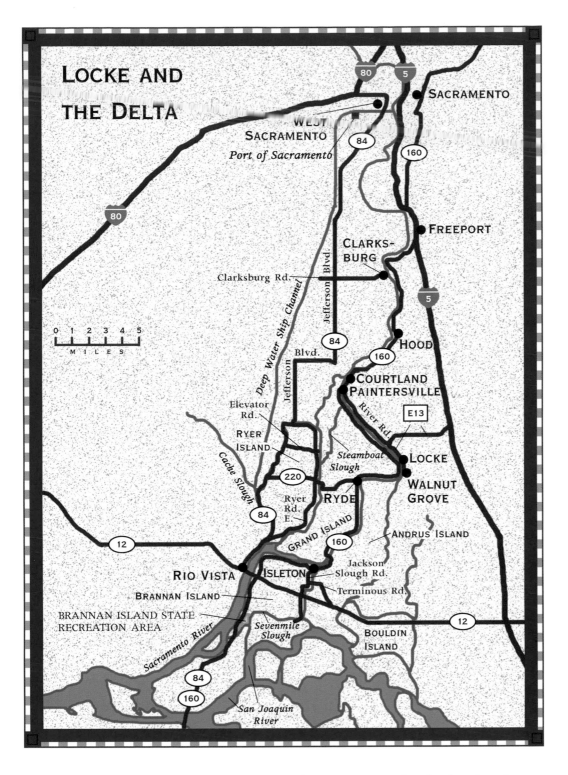

LOCKE AND THE DELTA

Isleton. It's easy to miss the turn, but it's still possible to reach Locke (albeit by longer routes), by turning right a few miles farther at Jackson Slough Road, or by turning north at Highway 160 a few miles after that.

Terminous Road circuitously follows the Georgiana Slough for a few miles and then veers left. At one time there were at least five canneries on the island. Today, the canneries have been replaced by resorts and marinas.

California Highway 160

A left turn at the north end of town quickly brought us to the impressively broad Sacramento River and Highway 160. The road-

CALIFORNIA SKETCH: JOHN SUTTER

Every child who grows up in California learns that gold was discovered in 1848 at Sutter's Mill, near Sacramento. They learn, too, that many fortunes were made during the ensuing gold rush. But most children don't know that John Sutter, the mill owner and the seminal figure in the history of California, lost his fortune because of the gold rush.

Johann August Suter was born on February 23, 1803, in the margraviate of Baden, an independent German state. Suter's ancestral homeland was just across the border of what is today Switzerland, and Suter considered himself to be Swiss. At the time of his birth, much of Switzerland was the French-controlled Helvetic Republic.

As a young man, Suter became an apprentice in a printing, publishing, and bookselling firm. After marrying, he changed the spelling of his name to John Augustus Sutter and began his own business ventures, but he soon ran up so many debts that he faced prison. At the age of thirty-one, married, and the father of four children, Sutter left his family and fled a police warrant and Europe for America. He would not see his wife for the next sixteen years.

Sutter settled in St. Louis, Missouri, where he apparently turned into something of a con man. A few years later he crossed the frontier into New Mexico as a trader on the Santa Fe Trail, where he came into contact with officials of the somewhat xenophobic Mexican government. He had also began to invent a new persona for himself, one that did not include mention of his family or debts in Europe.

He learned about Alta California, the Mexican province west of the Sierra Nevada Mountains and what is today simply California, while in New Mexico. Joining a party of fur trappers and missionaries, he took a circuitous route to reach his goal, traveling to Fort Vancouver, British Columbia; Honolulu in the Sandwich Islands, which we now call Hawaii; and Sitka, Alaska. From there, he sailed to Alta California, finally stepping ashore on July 1, 1839.

The Mexicans wanted to blunt the influx of Yankee fur trappers and settlers. The Mexican governor, Juan Alvarado, believed Sutter's hollow promise to instigate large-scale immigration of Swiss and German farmers into Alta California. Alvarado gave Sutter permission to explore and colonize the country east of present-day San Francisco.

Sutter named his colony New Helvetia. For the Swiss, the word Helvetia resonated then, as it does now, with mythic connotations. It was the name given by the Romans to western Switzerland, and "Helvetia" still appears on every Swiss postage stamp.

Sutter built a fort and supplied his new colony with food from a farm he established on the west bank of the Feather River. The farm was a few miles from the Sutter Buttes and the site of the present-day Yuba City.

Sutter's Fort became the hub of an empire and the destination for settlers arriving from Oregon or who had crossed the Sierra Nevada mountains. Sutter hired—some say enslaved—the Maidu to tend to his cattle and horses and to guard his fort. Sutter armed his fort with ordinance purchased from Fort Ross.

Despite his apparent success as a colonizer, Sutter had trouble controlling the financial aspects of his empire. His protégé, John Bidwell, wrote that Sutter was an especially soft touch who "had peculiar traits; his necessities compelled him to take all he could buy, and he paid all he could pay; but he failed to keep up with his payments. And so he soon found himself immensely—almost hopelessly—involved in debt." If we believe Bidwell, Sutter began many new enterprises not so much to enlarge his empire "as to find relief from his embarrassments."

Perhaps Sutter's empire would have collapsed of its own weight eventually, but the agent of destruction would not prove to be Sutter's poor business practices. Sutter's downfall came from the discovery of gold, made at Sutter's sawmill at the community of Coloma, near his fort. Gold-rush fever brought a stampede of miners who stripped New Helvetia of its animals and its tools and trampled its crops. Most, if not all of Sutter's workers and associates were caught up in the fever, too, and quickly deserted the fort.

Sutter's wife, Annette, came to California for the first time in 1850. The reunited family retreated from Sutter's Fort to a second home at Sutter's Feather River farm. For a few years, Sutter lived a quiet life, in the midst of his vineyards and orchards and gardens of rare plants. Meanwhile, squatters went to court and successfully invalidated portions of his Mexican land grant. In 1865, Sutter's house at the farm was destroyed by arson. It was the final California indignity.

Sutter and his wife moved to the little town of Lititz, Pennsylvania, where, though something of a recluse, he could enjoy the company of a number of Swiss expatriates.

The state of California granted Sutter a pension for his losses, and he hoped to receive similar help from the U.S. government. He died in Washington, D.C., two days after Congress adjourned without passing a bill that would have authorized a fifty-thousand-dollar payment to Sutter.

Sutter's remains were taken back to Lititz and interred in the Moravian Brother's Cemetery. Sutter, surrounded by other fallen Swiss, was finally at peace in the true New Helvetia.

ABOVE:

JOHN SUTTER, CIRCA 1865. (COURTESY OF CALIFORNIA STATE LIBRARY.)

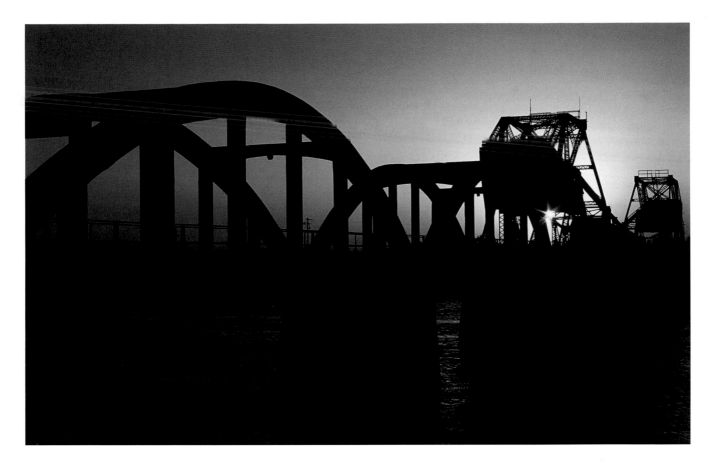

way here runs on top of the levee that holds the river back from Andrus Island. We turned right, continuing toward Locke.

Just north of Isleton, the Sacramento is crossed on a bascule bridge, a type of bridge that employs counterweights to part the span in the center, each end lifting up alternately to allow boats to pass. It's the same mechanical principle used in medieval times to raise and lower a castle drawbridge over a moat.

In addition to the bascule, there are two other types of bridges to watch for in the Delta. The more common is the swing bridge, with an arm that lifts up and down like a railroad crossing gate. The other is the less common vertical lift bridge, recognized by tall, twin towers. Like the bascule, vertical lift bridges use counterbalances, but the entire span raises as one unit.

We crossed the Sacramento on the bascule bridge and continued north on Highway 160. The Delta, though not far away from two major metropolitan areas, teems with wildlife. On the day we drove through,

turkey vultures floated above the fields. Great blue herons and egrets, looking more like pterodactyls than birds, soared over the river. I told my wife we were near the spot where I'd watched an American river otter cross the road in front of my car one night. At thirty-five to forty pounds, these aquatic mammals with rich brown fur look like a cross between a sea otter and a small seal. Although river otters may be the best swimmers of all American mammals, their four webbed feet make them less than athletic on land and many of them don't make it safely across the Delta roads. That night, though, I slowed my car, and the otter continued on its way unscathed.

Walnut Grove

About five miles north of the bridge at Isleton, the river makes a sweeping turn to the right and enters Walnut Grove. The town is one of the oldest along the Sacramento River, dating to 1850, when there were walnut forests in the area (the walnut trees, as well as virgin stands of oaks, were soon cut

THE SUN SETS BEHIND THE ISLETON BRIDGE, A BASCULE-TYPE SPAN THAT RAISES AND LOWERS LIKE A MEDIEVAL DRAWBRIDGE.

down to provide firewood for steamboats). By 1865, the town of Walnut Grove on the Sacramento had become a major shipping port for Bartlett pears; even today more pears are produced in the Delta than anywhere else in the world.

Spurred by its shipping industry, Walnut Grove was the only river town in the Delta to sit astride both the east and west riverbanks, and for a time the residential area was on the east bank, and the commercial district on the west. People traveled back and forth between the two banks by ferry until a bridge was built in 1916. The first bridge, since replaced by a modern span, was also the first bascule bridge west of the Mississippi River.

Below the levee on the east side of Wal-nut Grove, you will find the old Chinese and Japanese sections of the town, with a clutch of buildings—some occupied, some vacant—and several narrow, snaking streets.

The Chinese had settled in the quiet, relatively remote confines of the Delta after the goldfields had played out and after the transcontinental railroad was completed. The Chinese of Walnut Grove were largely free of the racial discrimination they faced in other parts of the state. But the Chinese community was not destined to stay in Walnut Grove, and, when Walnut Grove's Chinatown suffered a catastrophic fire in 1915, the conflagration provided the stimulus for the Chinese to build a town of their own.

Walnut Grove also had a smaller Japa-

A STATELY DELTA HOME.

nese community. When Chinatown burned, it was rebuilt and repopulated by an expanded Japanese population. Today, at least forty families of Japanese descent live east of the Japanese commercial area of Walnut Grove.

Locke

The town the Chinese built is only about a mile north of Walnut Grove. Locke was designed by Chinese architects and completed in 1920. The town was originally named Lockeport for George Locke, the owner of the land on which the buildings stand. The name of the town was later shortened.

Actually, the first building on the site of Locke went up in 1912, when businessman Chan Tin-San built a saloon on George Locke's property. Tin-San apparently understood the business potential of locating his saloon opposite a Southern Pacific Railroad wharf and warehouse. The wharf brought workers and the workers brought money to his saloon. Another man given credit by local historians for co-founding Locke was Bing Lee, who convinced several Chinese merchants to lease property from George Locke.

In the 1940s, farm workers and residents had a choice of restaurants, herb shops, grocery stores, fish markets, and boarding houses. Outsiders could rub elbows with the locals in gambling halls and bordellos. Today, Locke is long past its heyday. And that is precisely why Locke exudes so much unforced, authentically nostalgic charm. Recognizing this, the U.S. Interior Department placed Locke on the National Register of Historic Places in 1970.

On our trip through the Delta, Kathy and I followed the arch of the river on County Road E13 to reach Locke. We drove slowly past buildings whose second stories rose above the levee; here and there rickety wooden steps led down the sides of the buildings to Main Street, at the base of the levee. Across the highway we could see that Chan Tin-San was right about the old Southern Pacific warehouse, which over the years

ABOVE:
THE KEE SING STORE, WITH THE DAI LOY MUSEUM IN THE BACKGROUND, ALONG LOCKE'S MAIN STREET.

LEFT:
A DOG TAKING A LITTLE REST IN LOCKE.

A BOAT RESTS AT ANCHOR IN THE LOST SLOUGH, INVISIBLE BEHIND A LEVEE FROM NEARBY LOCKE.

The day we stopped in, there were more people sitting inside Al's than anywhere else in town. We decided to stay for lunch, and although Kathy declined to spread peanut butter on her chicken sandwich, I was more adventurous. Along with peanut butter, I added a healthy amount of apricot jelly to my steak sandwich. I enjoyed every unusual bite, but then, I like liver and onions, too.

After lunch we wandered through the Dai Loy Museum, once a bustling gambling house and now the official repository for all things historic in Locke, including Chinese gambling paraphernalia. After visiting the museum we walked behind Main Street. Making our way past houses and little gardens, we wandered no more than a few hundred yards to the base of another levee topped with trees. Scrambling up an almost indistinct trail, we viewed the Lost Slough on the far side of the levee, where pleasure boats sat at anchor in the still waters.

We returned to our car and traveled north again along River Road on the east side of the river. We passed some beautifully restored nineteenth-century homes, as well as countless pear orchards, before reaching Paintersville, where Highway 160 crosses the river again to follow the eastern levee, and then Courtland, home to a pear fair each July. Hood, perhaps the only town along the river that doesn't have a marina, is a short drive farther north. Clarksburg, settled in 1849, is visible on the west side of the river.

Just north of Freeport, on the outskirts of Sacramento, Highway 160 veers away from the river and crosses Interstate 5, where the suburbs of the state capital have closed in on the Sacramento River. The backroad blends into Freeport Boulevard and continues on to downtown Sacramento.

California Highway 84 to Ryer Island

Kathy and I got on Interstate 5 and drove into Sacramento proper, and continued our vacation for the next several days. On our return home, however, we made another trip through the Delta. This time we took Inter-

grew to be more than eight hundred feet long. More than a half dozen fruit packers once rented space in the building, but today the warehouse is used to store and launch pleasure boats.

There isn't a lot of parking space in Locke, either alongside County Road E13, or along the one block of Main Street. It's easier to find parking on the north side of town, near the former Locke School that now serves as an annex of the Dai Loy Museum. The museum itself is at the south end of town.

We strolled along the wooden boardwalks on Main Street. The paint on the storefronts has faded or peeled away, and some of the buildings seem to lean at precarious angles while many of the shops are vacant. Most of the Chinese residents are gone, too. Today, people live in apartments on Main Street or in houses on the southern and eastern ends of town.

Locke, moribund though it may appear, is still very much alive, with several shops, a grocery store, and the museum. And there's Al's Place, a bar and restaurant where patrons dine on the local specialties: steak or chicken with peanut butter. An unusual mural, gracing one wall, pictures Asian cowboys herding cattle.

FARM ALONG HIGHWAY
84 ON RYER ISLAND.

THE TOMATO HARVEST,
RYER ISLAND.

state 80 to West Sacramento and exited on Jefferson Boulevard (Highway 84). From Jefferson, we could see two cargo ships in the Port of Sacramento, most likely loading shipments of rice or fertilizer. The ships come up the Sacramento River out of the Bay Area and through the Deep Water Ship Channel on the west side of the Delta.

Jefferson Boulevard/Highway 84 heads south out of the city, lifting us up and over the no longer used Sacramento Lock, and down into mostly open farm country, with views northeast toward downtown Sacramento and west to the Deep Water Ship Channel levee. After a dozen miles, Highway 84 reaches Clarksburg Road on the left, giving quick access to the old river town by the same name.

Continuing on Highway 84 another ten miles led us to the north end of Ryer Island. The island can be circumnavigated via a wiggly, twenty-mile route. Two other roads, California Highway 220 and Elevator Road, cut across the interior of the island. There are a few resort harbors on the southeast end of Ryer, which is otherwise given over to farming. We crossed onto Ryer Island over an old swing bridge and turned right, continuing on Highway 84. We stopped to talk to a man and a woman who were sitting next to their bikes. They were from Sacramento, out for the afternoon on a ride along the long, flat stretches of the Delta backroads. Kathy and I envied their leisurely, almost effortless journey. If there's a good place to ride a bike, surely it's on quiet, perfectly level Ryer Island.

Highway 84 here was a particularly deserted stretch of road. To our left, the interior of the island was filled with groves of pear trees, cornfields, and farm buildings, some maintained, while others had fallen into disrepair. On our right, off the levee, the marshland was submerged for hundreds of yards beneath shallow water. Far beyond the marsh we could make out the levee that hid the Deep Water Ship Channel.

When we'd come about halfway around the circular route and reached the southern end of Ryer Island, we reached a ferry with neither fee nor cable. The ferry leads across Cache Slough and into the town of Rio Vista, where Highway 84 continues. In 1985, a humpback whale accidentally swam into San Francisco Bay and up into the Sacramento Delta, reaching as far as the southern end of Ryer Island. After a few weeks of international publicity, Humphrey the Wayward Whale was coaxed back into the Pacific Ocean.

We opted to continue circling Ryer rather than boarding this ferry, heading north on Ryer Road East. A few miles up the road, we reached another ferry that crosses Steamboat Slough to Grand Island. Pulled by a cable, this free ferry can carry about half a dozen cars at a time across the slough.

Heading for Home

This time we took the ferry, waiting our turn to board behind a UPS truck. I pulled to the front of the ferry, with the UPS truck next to me. As we started off with a little jolt across the slough, which used to serve as a shortcut for steamboats plying the Sacramento River, there was a perception that my car was rolling, and I had a sudden, overpowering urge to put my foot on the brake and steer my car. In a moment, the odd sensation passed, and soon we were safely on the other side of the slough.

Once on Grand Island we drove a short distance south, turning left onto Highway 220. We traversed Grand Island, traveling through miles of farmlands, finally coming out at the community of Ryde on the Sacramento River. The town is home of the Ryde Hotel, renovated as a riverside art deco bed-and-breakfast inn, complete with dining room, swimming pool, boat dock, and a nine-hole golf course that winds through a pear orchard. Kathy and I relaxed in the dining room, where we watched the river roll by and snacked on fried zucchini and Cajun fries. Back in the car, we turned right onto Highway 160. A short drive and a bridge over the river, soon brought us back to Isleton.

From Isleton, we followed Highway 160 about five miles, as far as the Brannan Island State Recreation Area. The island itself is named after the early Mormon pioneer, Sam Brannan. In 1846, shortly after his arrival in California, he explored the Delta with a band of Mormon followers. Brannan published San Francisco's first newspaper, led the construction of more than two hundred buildings in that city, and his shrewd business practices before and during the gold rush made him California's first millionaire.

There is a comfortable campground on Brannan Island at the State Recreation Area, complete with spacious lawns, showers, and easy access to the Sevenmile Slough for kayakers and canoeists. While camping on a previous trip to the Delta, I'd watched dawn turn the skies pink. The sun rose over neighboring Twitchell Island and Sevenmile

Slough to light a lone kayaker gliding silently across the water.

West of Brannan Island, along Highway 160, there is a good view of the confluence of the Sacramento and San Joaquin Rivers. My wife and I would have enjoyed spending the night on Brannan, but on this trip through the Delta, it was now time to head for home. We retraced our route back up Highway 160 to Highway 12 and drove east, back to Andrus Island and then onto Bouldin Island, where James Corwin had sweated on the dredges by day and swatted his millions of mosquitoes by night. Once off the Terminous Bridge we soon returned to Interstate 5 and its collection of fast food restaurants. We were sorry to leave the Delta, where time is suspended.

BUILT IN 1927, THE RYDE HOTEL ON GRAND ISLAND WAS A SPEAKEASY, RUMORED TO BE A BORDELLO, AND IS NOW AN ELEGANT BED-AND-BREAKFAST.

PART V

THE

CASCADE RANGE

Much of the rugged land-scape in northeastern California has been shaped by violent events rising from deep within the earth. Major high-ways and backroads lead around and even over spectacular volcanoes, whose enormous cones are topped with snowfields, glaciers, and lakes. Vast lava flows are here, too, some containing hollow lava tubes that extend for thousands of feet.

The volcanoes and lava flows in north-eastern California are part of the Cascade Range, which stretch from California north into British Columbia, Canada. The Cascades, together with the Klamath Mountains to the northwest, seal off the northern end of the Central Valley. The forested slopes of the Cascades average about 4,000 feet in eleva-tion, but many Cascade volcanoes rise to much greater heights, including two tower-ing volcanoes in California, Lassen Peak and Mount Shasta. Lassen Peak, near the south-ern edge of the Cascades, stands 10,457 feet above sea level. Mount Shasta, perhaps the most prominent mountain in the state be-cause of its height (14,162 feet) and because it stands in isolation from any other peak, is about an hour's drive north of Redding.

There are more than a thousand volca-noes in the Cascade Range between Lassen Peak and Mount Rainier, in Washington. At least seven of them have erupted since the latter portion of the eighteenth century and are considered to still be active, including Mount St. Helens in Washington, which erupted in 1980, and Lassen Peak, which erupted early in the twen-tieth century.

Cascade volcanoes owe their existence to the shifting crustal plates that ride over the earth's surface in the Pa-cific Northwest. In a process called subduc-tion, the denser plate of oceanic crust is forced beneath the lighter continental crust. High temperatures and pressures from the weight of the earth above partially melt the mantel underneath the continental crust, turning it into magma. Some of this magma then rises to the earth's surface where sub-sequent eruptions have given birth to the Cascade's chain of volcanoes. These volca-noes lie in a broad band generally parallel-ing the coastline, part of the "Ring of Fire," a roughly circular group of volcanoes located on islands, peninsulas, and edges of conti-nents along the rim of the Pacific Ocean.

There are three types of volcanoes in the Cascades. Mount Shasta is an example of a stratocone, or composite, volcano. These cone-shaped volcanoes stand as much as 8,000 feet above their bases and often have a crater at the summit with a central vent or a group of vents. The indispensable attribute of a composite volcano is a conduit or con-duit system, through which lava, cinders, ash, and other material can erupt. Lava, in particular, either flows through breaks in the

INSET:
LOGS AT THE ROSEBURG
LUMBER MILL IN WEED.

FACING PAGE:
HIGHWAY 89 WINDING
ITS WAY TOWARD
LASSEN PEAK.

crater wall or emanates from fissures on the flanks of the cone.

By contrast, Lassen Peak is a dome volcano, one of the largest in the world. A volcanic dome forms when magma is too viscous to flow out through a vent; most of the growth of the dome is internal. Lassen's periodic eruptions from 1914 to 1917 were unusual, because most dome volcanoes rarely produce more than one period of activity. Lassen Peak is only about 2,000 feet from its base to its summit, but it developed on top of an older, eroded stratocone, and so stands over 10,000 feet above sea level.

Shield volcanoes consist almost entirely of lava flows, and have broad, gently sloping cones that look like a Roman warrior's shield. The shield is slowly created over a long period of time from thousands of lava flows expelled out of the cone. These flows can extend over enormous distances. Lava can also erupt from vents along fissures in the flanks of the cone.

Many shield volcanoes in California and Oregon are 1,500 to 2,000 feet in elevation and three to four miles in diameter. They aren't nearly as dramatic in appearance as the enormous stratocones like Shasta. However, some of the world's largest volcanoes are shield volcanoes. Mauna Loa in Hawaii, the largest shield volcano in the world, stands 13,677 feet above sea level, not counting the additional 15,000 feet of submerged mountain that rises from the ocean floor. Medicine Lake Volcano, about thirty miles east of Mount Shasta, is a good example of a shield volcano in the Cascade Range.

TALES OF MOUNT SHASTA

Mount Shasta is not, at 14,162 feet above sea level, the highest peak in California. That honor goes to Mount Whitney, at 14,445 feet. But Mount Shasta may be the most impressive mountain in the state, rising over its surrounding terrain in spectacular isolation from any other peak. Mount Shasta, associated with a number of unusual legends, is a lodestone for naturalists, photographers, occultists, and mountaineers.

The Town of Mount Shasta to Weed

My wife and I arrived in the early evening one summer, at the town of Mount Shasta,

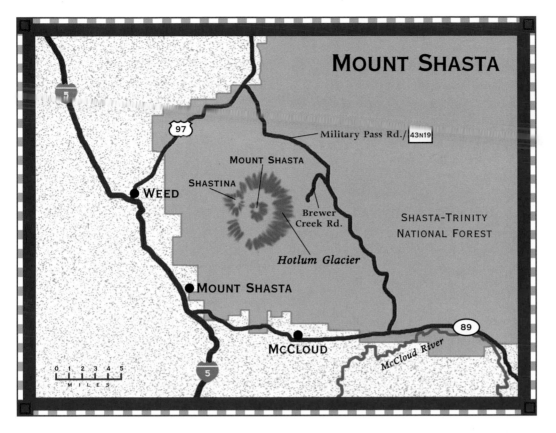

MOUNT SHASTA

5

97

Military Pass Rd. / 43N19

MOUNT SHASTA

SHASTINA

WEED

Brewer
Creek Rd.

SHASTA-TRINITY
NATIONAL FOREST

Hotlum Glacier

MOUNT SHASTA

McCLOUD

89

McCloud River

0 1 2 3 4 5
M I L E S

5

MOUNT SHASTA AND
SHASTINA PEAK, A
SUBSIDIARY PEAK ON
SHASTA'S WESTERN
FLANK, RISE BEHIND
HIGHWAY 97, NORTH OF
WEED.

ONE OF THE PIECES
FROM THE LIVING
MEMORIAL SCULPTURE
GARDEN ALONG U.S. 97.

turing a few spectacular viewpoints of the mountain. Because we had our dog with us, we ordered Mexican food from a nearby restaurant and sat down for dinner at a table in Lonna's plant-filled backyard.

After dinner we walked north a couple of blocks, and watched the sun set over the mountain. The town is thirty-five hundred feet in elevation, and the peak towered more than ten thoudand feet above us.

The next morning we lingered a bit over coffee and the newspaper. We packed a lunch before driving north toward the town of Weed, eight miles away on busy Interstate 5. We exited Interstate 5 onto Weed Boulevard, glad to be off the freeway, and traveled along Main Street with its quaint storefronts. We continued north through town to view the impressive Roseburg lumber mill, stacked with thousands of logs and finished boards, with Mount Shasta towering in the background.

Weed to Hotlum Glacier

We continued to the north end of town and merged onto U.S. Highway 97. We drove about thirteen miles to view the Living Memorial Sculpture Garden, dedicated to all veterans. The garden contains ten stylized metal sculptures of soldiers, nurses, and prisoners of war. More than fifty-eight thousand trees surround the garden, one for each American killed in the Vietnam War.

We retraced our way along U.S. 97, and turned left onto Military Pass Road. Built in 1857, the road provided a route from Shasta Valley, which lies west of Mount Shasta, to Fort Crook, which was northeast of the mountain. We followed the good dirt road over the northwest slopes of Mount Shasta, driving past pines and sage and manzanita.

Military Pass Road, also designated as Forest Service Road 43N19, led us steeply up toward the northwest face of the mountain. Shastina, a subsidiary peak that was built up over the last ten thousand years on Shasta's flank, was impressive in its own right. Looking back down the mountain, we

where California Highway 89 and Interstate 5 meet. The town is at the southwestern base of Mount Shasta, an ancient, inactive volcano that last erupted about two hundred years ago.

Our intent was to circumnavigate the mountain the next day. But that night, we relaxed at the Dream Inn, a comfortable Victorian bed-and-breakfast on Chestnut Street, a block east of Main Street. Our hostess, Lonna Smith, graciously gave us a tour fea-

enjoyed a tremendous view of Shasta Valley, spread out to the west. To the north, the Cascade highlands rose to cut off our view into Oregon, only about twenty miles away.

Deep in the forest, but still able to see Shasta rising above the pines, we reached Forest Service Road 19, which is a wider and better-graded dirt road than 43N19. Turning left would have taken us back to U.S. 97, north of Military Pass Road. But we continued driving southeast on 43N19, past occasional meadows, logging roads, and more stands of pines.

Coming around the east side of the mountain we passed rough Brewer Creek Road, which some friends and I had traveled over many years before to reach a trail leading up to the glacier-covered, upper slopes of Mount Shasta. From just below the Hotlum Glacier, one of five glaciers on the mountain, my climbing friends and I had watched the shadow of the volcano fall across the Medicine Lake Highlands to the east.

A Shasta Flashback

Well before dawn the next morning those many years ago, my companions and I were up and out of our sleeping bags to begin our ascent of the mountain. We strapped crampons—little spikes—to the bottom of our boots to help us gain purchase on the icy glacier. As we began to climb, I picked up my ice axe to help me keep my balance on the steep slopes, and to help bring me to a halt if I slipped.

Dawn broke to the east and the sun threatened to rise over the bulge of Medicine Lake Volcano. The top of our volcano, a massive stratocone built up over the course of one hundred thousand years, was still invisible to us.

So were the Lemurians, the mysterious

TOWERING MOUNT SHASTA, ALL 14,162 FEET OF IT, STANDS ALONE IN THE SHASTA NATIONAL FOREST, THE GLACIERS ON ITS EAST FACE REFLECTING THE LIGHT OF AN EARLY MORNING SUN.

beings that many people believe inhabit the interior of Shasta. The Lemurians are said to live in caves lined with veins of gold. According to some disciples of the occult, the Lemurians are as much as seven feet tall.

My friends and I finally reached the top of Mount Shasta. There was no sign of the pancake-shaped cloud, called a lenticular, that often hovers over the top of Shasta. Some people speculate that these odd clouds are flying saucers.

Hundreds of people ascend Mount Shasta each year. John Muir, the naturalist who founded the Sierra Club, and his climbing companion, Jerome Fay, ascended the peak on April 30, 1875. They were caught on the summit by a snowstorm and had to seek refuge at the base of the summit pinnacle, where they managed to survive by sitting in a sulfurous hot spring.

On that earlier mountaineering trip, we reached our base camp as a lenticular cloud began to form over the summit of the peak we had just climbed. On the way down, we listened for the sound of the bells made at the City of Yaktavia, which is said to exist deep inside the mountain. The Yaktavians of the Secret Commonwealth of Mount Shasta are reputedly the greatest bell makers in the world. Thousands of these bells can sometimes be heard along stretches of the highways around the mountain. But on our climbing trip all we heard was the rising of the wind.

Back to the Town of Mount Shasta

On our present trip, Kathy and I, after twenty-five miles of dirt road, regained pavement. For now, Shasta was hidden be-

hind trees, but we were compensated for the loss of the view by the sight of a deer with her two fawns, who stood motionless next to the road.

Following the pavement for about ten miles, we reached Highway 89 where we turned right, now on the southeast side of Mount Shasta. The little lumber town of McCloud was a few miles to the west. Along the way, we made a detour to explore the McCloud River and three waterfalls. The well-graded dirt road, passing through a lush forest of pines and ferns, more or less paralleled Highway 89 just to the north.

We spent a little time exploring the town of McCloud. Like Weed, McCloud owes its

THE MCCLOUD RIVER WINDS THROUGH THE SHASTA NATIONAL FOREST, PARALLELING HIGHWAY 89 TO THE NORTH.

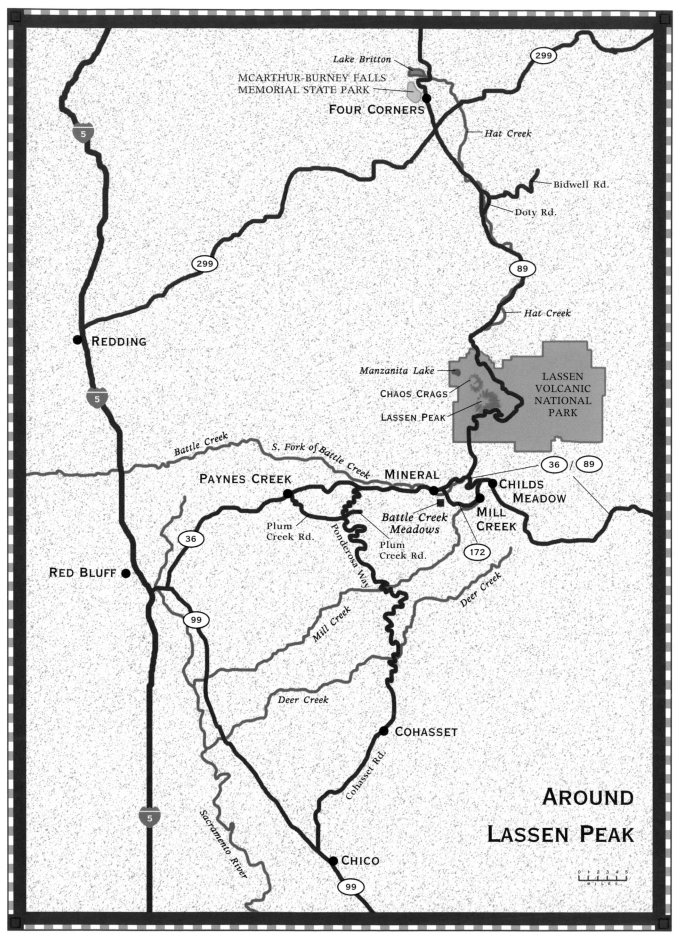

Lake Britton

McARTHUR-BURNEY FALLS
MEMORIAL STATE PARK

FOUR CORNERS

299

Hat Creek

Bidwell Rd.

Doty Rd.

5

299

89

Hat Creek

REDDING

5

Manzanita Lake

CHAOS CRAGS

LASSEN PEAK

LASSEN
VOLCANIC
NATIONAL
PARK

Battle Creek

S. Fork of Battle Creek

MINERAL

36 / 89

PAYNES CREEK

**CHILDS
MEADOW**

Plum
Creek Rd.

*Battle Creek
Meadows*

**MILL
CREEK**

36

Ponderosa Way

Plum
Creek Rd.

172

RED BLUFF

99

Mill Creek

Deer Creek

Deer Creek

COHASSET

Cohasset Rd.

AROUND

LASSEN PEAK

Sacramento River

CHICO

99

0 1 2 3 4 5
MILES

existence to the lumber industry. Unlike Weed, McCloud was a company town. Until 1965, the homes and businesses were owned and run by the McCloud River Lumber Company.

We visited the McCloud Hotel, restored to its original 1915 elegance in recent years, and the train yard of the McCloud River Railroad, which is up the hill from the center of town. The railway carries lumber along its tracks east of Shasta. During the tourist season, passengers can ride the train, too.

Kathy and I drove the final twelve miles from McCloud to the town of Mount Shasta, ending our circumnavigation of the mountain. On the way back to the Dream Inn, we watched a lenticular cloud form over the top of the mountain, and listened in vain for the bells of Yaktavia.

Around Lassen Peak

There are two stories to tell here about the roads around Lassen Peak. One begins before history was recorded on paper, and ends a little after the beginning of the twentieth century. The other story unfolds almost a century later.

The Native Americans who inhabited the Cascade Range south of Lassen Peak for thousands of years referred to themselves simply as the Yahi, "the people." There were about three hundred Yahi when the gold rush began in 1848. Fifteen years later, hunted by settlers, the Yahi faced annihilation. A few members of the tribe sought refuge in a nearly impenetrable wilderness where they and their ancestors survived almost undetected into the twentieth century.

Mineral and Mill Creek

One summer afternoon, my wife Kathy and I made a trip to Yahi country starting in Red Bluff, a town in the northern Central Valley. Exiting Interstate 5, we drove east on California Highway 36 over the broad, tree-lined Sacramento River and up through oak-dotted foothills toward Lassen Peak.

LASSEN PEAK, ITS SUMMIT RISING 10,457 FEET ABOVE SEA LEVEL, LOOMS ABOVE MANZANITA LAKE ON THE NORTHWESTERN SLOPE OF THE MOUNTAIN.

ABOVE:
CHAOS JUMBLES, THE
REMNANTS OF A
CENTURIES-OLD
ROCKSLIDE, LITTERS THE
LANDSCAPE BELOW
CHAOS CRAGS, JUST
EAST OF HIGHWAY 89.

RIGHT:
THE CASCADE MOUN-
TAINS SOUTH OF LASSEN
PEAK, VIEWED FROM
CHILDS MEADOW, ALONG
HIGHWAY 36/89.

The mountain, named for gold rush pioneer Peter Lassen, is the southernmost major volcano in the Cascades. Lassen Peak last erupted in 1917 and is still considered active. The Yahi inhabited the land from Lassen Peak west, to the fringe of the Central Valley, and south, to Deer Creek.

We reached the little resort community of Mineral, forty-three miles east of Red Bluff, and four miles shy of the Highway 89 turnoff to Lassen Volcanic National Park. We stopped for iced tea at Mineral Lodge, which was built by the Hampton family and has been in operation since 1880. Sitting on the front porch, we listened to diners speak at least two languages other than our own and watched with admiration as several members of a bicycle club pedaled up to the lodge.

Rather than continuing on Highway 36 toward Lassen Peak, we traveled onto California Highway 172, which begins just across the road from the lodge and circles back to Highway 36 over nine miles. Highway 172 was the original route of Highway 36, which was built in the 1930s. The old road headed south through Battle Creek Meadows, which we found to be filled with wild Shasta daisies and Indian paintbrush. It crossed over the south fork of Battle Creek, named for a bloody fight in 1854 between trappers and Native Americans, quite possibly the Yahi. Beyond the meadow, Highway 172 contoured over heavily forested ridges to reach Mineral Summit, the highest point along the highway, before dropping steeply to parallel Mill Creek. The terrain was level here, and we drove past a forest service campground and rustic Mill Creek Resort, which was first opened in 1924.

The Yahi, also known as both the Mill Creek and Deer Creek Indians because they lived near those places, were apparently not well loved by the miners and settlers or even other tribes. In 1865 a large number of Yahi men, women, and children were ambushed and killed at Mill Creek, and from then on they were a doomed people.

The remaining, ever-dwindling number of Yahi were rarely encountered by whites over the next thirty-eight years, as they lived as exiles in a self-imposed Stone Age. They secreted themselves for fifteen years in the country around Mill Creek. When settlers like the Hamptons moved too close, the Yahi moved south, to Deer Creek, abandoning the area of Lassen Peak forever.

Childs Meadow to Lassen Volcanic National Park

Kathy and I wanted to stay at the Mill Creek Resort, which has several cabins, a store, and a private campground. But the cabins were taken, and we weren't in the right frame of mind to camp this night, so we followed the now less convoluted California Highway 172 a little farther. We passed by Mill Creek Meadows, green with summer grass, and rejoined Highway 36, which shares the roadway here with Highway 89. A right turn took us about a mile to the Childs Meadow Resort, where we did secure a room. While sitting outside at a picnic table and preparing dinner on a little camp stove, we enjoyed the sunset over the meadow and Brokeoff Mountain, an ancient volcano near Lassen Peak.

The next morning we drove west, stopping to look up Mill Creek for a spectacular view of Lassen Peak. We continued past the Highway 172 junction and drove another three miles to the base of Morgan Mountain. Highway 36 continued straight ahead, toward the towns of Mineral and Red Bluff. Highway 89 split off here to the right, winding its way up the southern slopes of Lassen Peak.

We turned right, toward the mountain. It's twenty-nine miles from the south side of the volcano to the north, on Lassen Peak Road, which loops around three sides of Lassen Peak. But, once winter snows arrive, the road can be closed for many months. Due to heavy snowfall in 1998, the road didn't open completely until July. The road offers access to five campgrounds, as well as several hiking trails and lakes. Also along the side of the road, many volcanic and geothermal features are visible, including hot springs, boiling mud pots, and steaming fumaroles, or volcanic vents.

That night, Kathy and I camped at Manzanita Lake, on the northwestern slopes of the mountain. We watched the sunset from the boulder field at Chaos Jumbles, the remnants of an immense rockslide that occurred three hundred years ago. Chaos Crags, a massive cliff above the boulders, erupted into existence about one thousand years ago, no doubt making an impression on the Native Americans in the region.

Lassen Peak itself began to erupt in May of 1914. The most massive eruption occurred in 1915, when a mushroom cloud reached six miles into the sky and sent broad rivers of lava north and east of the mountain. The last eruption came two years later, though ash and steam (but no lava), continued to vent sporadically until 1921.

There were no Yahi near Lassen Peak in 1915. But one Yahi man was still alive elsewhere.

Deer Creek

In November, 1908, a party of surveyors exploring along Deer Creek spotted a naked man standing on a rock next to the water, holding a long spear, but the man quickly fled. Later, the surveyors found what appeared to be a Native American camp. As they drew close, they watched a middle-aged woman helping an old man escape into the scrub oak. An old woman, unable to walk, was found under some blankets in the camp. The surveyors tried to reassure the woman they meant no harm, although they did remove the contents of the camp, including bows and arrows and skin blankets, things the last-known Yahi needed to survive. The interlopers left the woman and returned to their own camp for dinner. When they returned the next day, the woman was gone.

From Manzanita Lake, Kathy and I explored along Highway 89 to the north. We followed the course of Hat Creek, and when we reached Doty Road, we turned right and then right again on Bidwell Road. We drove a few miles to the Hat Creek Radio Observatory, where several gleaming dishes listen to the heavens. From our perch below the dishes, we had a panoramic view of the surrounding landscape, including Lassen Peak to the south, and Mount Shasta to the north.

We returned to Highway 89 and contin-

ASTRONOMERS AT THE HAT CREEK RADIO OBSERVATORY, ON BIDWELL ROAD NORTH OF LASSEN PEAK, STUDY THE ORIGINS AND NATURE OF THE UNIVERSE BY LISTENING TO RADIO FREQUENCIES.

ued north, as far as beautiful McArthur-Burney Falls Memorial State Park, six miles past the Highway 299 junction. The park sits at an elevation of thirty-two hundred feet. It has a large campground, and it provides easy access to the adjacent Lake Britton, a reservoir built by Pacific Gas and Electric in 1923 to supply power to the Central Valley, which also serves boaters and anglers.

However, the chief reason to visit the park is to see Burney Falls, named after Samuel Burney, an early pioneer who was killed in 1859, perhaps by a band of Pit River Indians. The story with its details shrouded in mystery is a real whodunit that eludes a solution by historians.

Although the falls are named after Mr. Burney, half the park is named for the McArthur family, which purchased the land around the falls in 1919 and then donated it to the state.

We paid the nominal entry fee for the day, and parked the car near the start of the trail leading to the falls. We were rewarded, after just a few yards, with a wonderful view of the falls from above. The water drops 129 feet from the top of the falls into a pool below.

Burney Falls is an unusual waterfall. Water flows over the edge of the falls, like any other waterfall, but water also flows through the substructure of the falls, shooting out of the cliff about halfway down. It does this because the material over which the water flows is rhyolite, a porous volcanic rock.

The falls are unusual for another reason: water continues to flow at the same rate all year long, the subterranean rock perpetually gorged with rainwater and snowmelt. Some 100 million gallons of water spill over the top or leak out the middle of the falls every day.

Kathy and I walked down the trail. Over the next few hundred yards, the way led down gentle switchbacks to the edge of the pool opposite the base of the falls. Kathy and I noticed that the temperature near the bottom of the canyon was several degrees cooler

than the temperature at the top of the trail. We spent several minutes enjoying the scene and letting the mist from the falls blow over us. Then we returned to the top of the falls, a bit reluctant to leave the cool depths of the canyon for the warmer world above.

From the state park we returned to the Central Valley and Redding via Highway 299.

I would make another journey into Yahi country the following spring, this time driving northeast on Cohasset Road from the town of Chico. The road led past canyons choked with scrub oak, then continued up into the pine-covered mountains. I reached the little community of Cohasset, where the

THE DEEPLY RUTTED PONDEROSA WAY, WHICH SERVES AS BOTH A LOGGING ROAD AND THE SOUTHERN ROUTE INTO THE ISHI WILDERNESS, CATCHES THE LIGHT FROM THE SETTING SUN.

only services were a gas station and small general store. Several miles further, Cohasset Road ended where the pavement became dirt. The new road, Ponderosa Way, continued to climb and snaked around the southern and eastern edges of the Ishi Wilderness.

I discovered that, for the first few miles, Ponderosa Way is used by logging trucks, so there were deep ruts in the road that had to be carefully navigated. But the ruts ended where the road dropped abruptly toward Deer Creek. There was a panoramic view of the rugged Ishi Wilderness, a designated wilderness within the Lassen National Forest, with Lassen Peak a snow-covered speck in the far distance. As I surveyed this vast, remote land, it was easy to understand how the Yahi had remained hidden from the rest of the world for so long.

Ponderosa Way reached Deer Creek, passed a few primitive campgrounds, and continued to Plum Creek Road, which, to the west, eventually joined Highway 36 at the little community of Paynes Creek. From there, the way led quickly down the mountain to Red Bluff and the modern world.

Three years after the Yahi were discovered at Deer Creek, a middle-aged American Indian man, wearing only an old undershirt, walked up to a slaughterhouse about four miles from the town of Oroville, far to the south of Yahi country. He was starving and had tried to steal some meat. The employees of the slaughterhouse called the sheriff, who, unable to communicate with the man, put him in a jail cell reserved for the insane.

He was, of course, one of the Yahi the surveyors had seen. No trace of the other Yahi was found, and it is believed they likely died soon after their discovery at Deer Creek. The lone survivor was soon taken to live at the Museum of Anthropology in San Francisco until his death in 1916.

Before the last Yahi died, he willingly shared his knowledge of his culture with the anthropologists with whom he lived. But following the custom of his people, he never shared his actual name with his rescuers. He was known simply by the Yahi word for a man, Ishi.

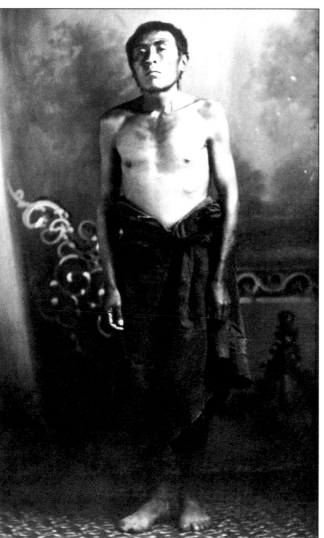

PART VI

THE GREAT BASIN DESERT

First Native Americans, then the Spanish, and then American fur trappers pushed their way into the Great Basin, a complex, rugged, and dry region of mountain ranges and desert valleys. Formed by a series of earth movements along fault lines that run mostly north and south, the Great Basin stretches east to the Wasatch Range near Salt Lake City, Utah, and west into eastern California, touching the base of the Sierra Nevada Mountains.

Created by the rain shadow of the Cascade and Sierra Nevada Mountains to the west, and the rain shadow created by the Rockies to the east, the Great Basin Desert roughly fills the Great Basin. It is the largest of the four North American deserts (the others are the Mojave, the Sonoran, and the Chihuahuan).

The rivers in the Great Basin Desert have no outlet to the sea. Rivers such as the Humboldt in Nevada often dry up as they cross the desert. Or they empty into large lakes, which during dry years can also dry up.

The Great Basin, more than four thousand feet in average elevation, is a cold desert where snow falls during the winter, and where temperatures can dip below freezing for more than a week at a time. Inhospitable though the land may be to humans, it is a fine home for rabbits, bobcats, coyotes, and pronghorn, which are sometimes incorrectly called antelopes.

After the Lewis and Clark Expedition of 1806 traveled from Saint Louis to the Pacific Ocean, a fantastic rumor took hold that a large river, named the Buenaventura, crossed the desert from the Rockies to the Pacific and was deep enough to float a ship full of pioneers between its wide banks. The precise location of this waterway was not known.

It took the famous explorer John C. Fremont to shatter the myth of the "undiscovered" Buenaventura. Fremont, who named the Great Basin, announced to the world in 1844 that no river system flowed through the interior of the United States. Fremont also discovered the Humboldt River, which he named for Baron Alexander von Humboldt, a German explorer. The Humboldt, and not the Buenaventura, served as the route through part of Nevada. Most of those who came to California during the gold rush followed Fremont's path on their way west.

INSET:
PAINTERLY VIEW OF BODIE, LOOKING THROUGH A LEADED-GLASS WINDOW FROM THE STANDARD CONSOLIDATED STAMP MILL.

FACING PAGE:
A HALF-MOON RISES EARLY OVER THE BODIE SCHOOLHOUSE.

BODIE

Ghost towns, ever an endangered species of the American West, are subject to the vicissitudes of old age on the one hand and vandals on the other. One of the most impressive ghost towns, which goes by the somewhat funny sounding name of Bodie (it rhymes with "toady"), reposes peacefully on the western fringe of the Great Basin, east of the Sierra Nevada Mountains.

Early Days in Bodie

It might have a funny name, but there's nothing funny about Bodie's history. It was reputedly the most dangerous town in America in the 1870s when, on average, at least one person a day died in a shootout or knife fight, from overdosing on alcohol or opium, or in a mining accident.

Gold was Bodie's lure, discovered by Waterman S. Body (also known as William S. Bodey) in 1859. The change in spelling of the town's name was later made to ensure proper pronunciation. Body froze to death while bringing supplies to his claim, dying before the town that was named for him was built. In its heyday, over ten thousand people called Bodie home.

The gold was hauled out of mine shafts sunk deep into the surrounding mountains. Eventually, enormous stamp mills, which crushed the rocks and boulders to extract the gold, operated twenty-four ear-splitting hours a day. After

1889, as the gold became depleted, the town began to die. The last residents left Bodie in 1962 when the state took over the town.

Bodie is now a state historic park and is open year-round; a small entrance fee is charged. At more than eight thousand feet above sea level, Bodie is nestled in a high desert valley formed by a spur range of the Sierra Nevada Mountains. There are no accommodations or campgrounds, no gas stations or souvenir stands, and not so much as a Coke machine. Snow can and often does close the roads, usually from November through May, when the only way to reach the park is on skis or by snowmobile.

Backroads to Bodie

When the routes to the ghost town aren't blocked by snow, Bodie is easy to reach by car. The main road into town, California Highway 270, intersects U.S. Highway 395 about ten miles south of the resort town of Bridgeport. It's thirteen miles to Bodie, and all but the last three miles are paved.

There are two other ways to reach Bodie.

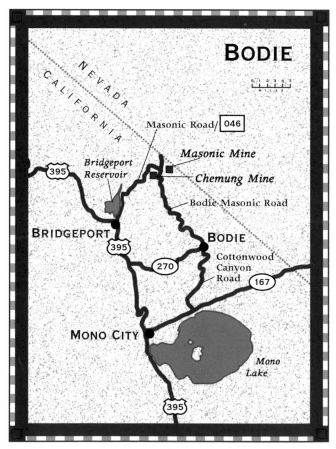

A SHEEPHERDER AND HIS FLOCK IN A HIGH DESERT MEADOW ALONG HIGHWAY 270 ON THE WAY TO BODIE.

One is via Cottonwood Canyon Road, which begins south of Bodie and runs very close to the northern shore of Mono Lake. Cottonwood Canyon provides a steeper, shorter, rougher route into the park, but the mostly dirt road does see less snow than Highway 270. Cottonwood can be reached by turning east off of U.S. 395 and onto Highway 167. The intersection is at Mono City.

The third route to Bodie is my favorite, although it involves a much longer approach and is completely on dirt. Begin about seven miles north of the little resort town of Bridgeport, and just north of the Bridgeport Reservoir. Turn east off of U.S. 395 onto Masonic Road, which is also signed as Forest Service Road 046. The road makes its way up through desert country onto more forested lands, reaching the abandoned Chemung Mine about nine miles from U.S. 395. The mine buildings are dilapidated and dangerous to enter, so exercise caution when poking around the site.

The junction with Bodie Masonic Road is a few miles past the Chemung Mine. This is a good place to watch for pronghorns. I once followed a female pronghorn up the side of a ridge, close enough to hear her breathing heavily in the thin air. I felt a bit silly, but I put my hands up next to my head, like horns, and pretended that I was a pronghorn, too, and made my way up the rough slope of the ridge. I don't think the pronghorn was fooled, and soon after reaching the ridge top, she disappeared over the other side.

The Masonic Mine is also near here. To view the ruins, stay left on Masonic Road. It's a mile or so to the mine, which sits at the bottom of a hill dotted with aspens.

Back on the Bodie Masonic Road, the route climbs and drops repeatedly before reaching a plateau. Here, the road begins a final, long descent into Bodie, about twenty-seven miles from U.S. 395.

Bodie comes into view as the road contours around a hillside. Although 85 percent of the town burned to the ground in two fires, the first in 1892, the last in 1935, Bodie

ABOVE:
ASPEN IN FALL COLOR NEAR THE MASONIC MINE.

LEFT:
THE TONGUE OF A FREIGHT WAGON RESTS ON THE MAIN STREET BOARDWALK AT BODIE STATE HISTORIC PARK.

A FIRST VIEW OF BODIE. THE STANDARD CONSOLIDATED STAMP MILL, WHICH PROCESSED GOLD, IS THE LARGE BUILDING IN THE BACKGROUND; THE TWO-STORY SCHOOLHOUSE IS ON THE FAR LEFT.

has over five hundred standing—or nearly standing—structures, including stores, hotels, a saloon, a barber shop, the schoolhouse, outhouses, a mill, and private homes, making it the largest ghost town in America.

Bodie Today

Today, the danger to Bodie's survival as a ghost town comes from souvenir hunters; board by board and brick by brick, vandals have severely damaged almost every other ghost town that once existed in the western United States. Park rangers, with the help of infrared burglar alarms, try to keep the tourists honest at Bodie.

During the summer, park docents lead tours of some of Bodie's buildings. Visitors are told that Bodie exists in a state of "arrested decay," and they are asked not to touch anything, lest they leave even fingerprints. Even without a tour, it's possible to peer through windows and see hope chests and china sets, schoolbooks, coffins, and a roulette table in the saloon where gambling was conducted illegally, but openly, until 1952.

The only people who stay overnight in Bodie are the rangers and maintenance workers. I skied into Bodie on my first visit during a winter when the snow was especially deep. My companions and I enjoyed a tour led by the two year-round resident rangers. We were, in fact, the only tourists in Bodie. The rangers told us that they had never seen

any ghosts, but said they had heard odd noises late at night, noises they declined to investigate. They also told us stories about two women, both murdered in the previous century, who had been seen and heard at the upstairs windows of two buildings in recent years. If true, Bodie, the town with the funny-sounding name, is indeed a ghost town.

LATE AFTERNOON IN THE GREAT BASIN DESERT GHOST TOWN OF BODIE.

PART VII

THE
SIERRA NEVADA

From the Cascade Range in the north to the Tehachapi Mountains in the south, the Sierra Nevada stretches like a giant spine along the eastern edge of California, four hundred miles in length and fifty miles wide. The Rocky Mountains, which reach from Alaska to New Mexico, are made up of several mountain chains, the longest less than two hundred miles long. Thus the Sierra Nevada is the longest, unbroken mountain chain in North America.

Much of the Sierra Nevada consists of an enormous block of igneous rock called a batholith by geologists. The Sierra Nevada began to uplift more than 10 million years ago. As it rose, the top of the batholith tilted from east to west. Its western slopes angled gently toward the inland sea that is now the Central Valley; its steep eastern face stands in places today more than fourteen thousand feet above sea level.

The original sedimentary rocks that underlay the Sierra (also known as the Sierras) were recrystallized into metamorphic rocks by molten magma rising from deep within the earth. While the magma pulsed and then cooled underground over the course of 100 million years, veins of quartz, some laden with gold, snaked through the fractures in the metamorphic and igneous rocks. The Sierra might have once extended considerably north, but a gigantic segment of the mountains broke off about 130 million years ago and began to slide, halting its migration sixty miles west. This segment became the Klamath Mountains.

Over the millennia, glaciers, rivers, and streams cut east and west across the Sierra. Lodgepole, sugar, and ponderosa pines grew on the upper slopes; oaks and maples at lower elevations; and Douglas fir, incense cedar, aspen, and giant sequoias in the midranges. Black bears, cougars, bobcats, bighorn sheep, lynx, marmots, and raccoons trod the mountains, as did grizzly bears and wolves—both of which are no longer found in California. Rainbow and cutthroat trout swam in the streams, and owls, hawks, eagles, and condors flew overhead.

The first human visitors and inhabitants to the Sierra were American Indians. Tribes of the Yokut, Maidu, and Miwok lived on the green, lower western slopes of the Sierra, and the Washoe and Mono tribes lived on the more desertlike east side.

On April 2, 1776, a Franciscan monk, Fray Pedro Font, viewed the snow-covered peaks of the Sierra from Mount Diablo, on

INSET:
THE HEADLIGHT OF A 1942 ISSUE LUMBER TRUCK AT THE SCHUTT LUMBER MILL IN GREELEY HILL.

FACING PAGE:
THE WINTER SUN BREAKS THROUGH THE CLOUDS, ILLUMINATING THE GRANITE FACE OF EL CAPITAN IN YOSEMITE NATIONAL PARK.

the west side of the Central Valley. His was the first written account of the Sierra, and he gave the range its name, *"una gran sierra nevada,"* grand, jagged, snowy mountains. Font wasn't the first European to view the mountains, that honor going in 1772 to two priests attached to the Gaspar de Portola expedition, which also discovered San Francisco Bay. But Font was the first to note the location of the Sierra Nevada on a map, and the first to give the mountains a written name. There have been other names. Native Americans described the mountain peaks as "snow upon snow, rock upon rock," and, much later, John Muir called them the "Range of Light."

The eastern escarpment of the Sierra was not penetrated by white men until the nineteenth century. Jedediah Strong Smith made the first transcontinental crossing, via the Great Basin Desert, arriving in Southern California in 1826. The following year, he made the first west to east crossing of the Sierra Nevada. Other explorers, such as Joseph Walker, Jim Beckwourth, John Bidwell, Kit Carson, and John Fremont, found their way across the rugged passes, too. Settlers made the arduous journey from the east, first on foot, later with their wagons via the crude roads they built over the crest of the mountains. During the gold rush, miners poured across the Sierra.

The transcontinental railroad crossed the Sierra in 1869. But even now, more than 150 years after Jedediah Strong Smith made his crossing, only a few passes (most of them closed in the winter), allow unfettered traffic in and out of California.

LAKE TAHOE

The Washoe were the first people to explore "Da-ow-a-ga," an enormous alpine lake in the northern Sierra Nevada Mountains. The explorer John Fremont and his scout, Christopher "Kit" Carson, may have been the first non-Indians to see Da-ow-a-ga in 1844. Fremont originally named the lake after Aime Jacques Alexander Bonpland, a French bota-

nist, but by 1862, the lake was given the name we use today, Lake Tahoe, a phonetic approximation of the original Washoe name.

Truckee to Tahoe City

Mark Twain, looking down on Lake Tahoe, described it as "a noble sheet of blue water lifted six thousand three hundred feet above the level of the sea, and walled in by a rim of snowclad mountain peaks three thousand feet higher still!" But a close-up look at the lake can be something of a disappointment for those who enjoy scenic byways. At least it was for me as I drove past motels, condominium complexes, gas stations, restaurants, and marinas that line much of Lake Tahoe's shoreline.

But even with the commercial development, Lake Tahoe remains the noble sheet of blue water that Twain first saw. Swimmers, boaters, and water-skiers enjoy the near crystal clear water in summer, and the mountainous wilderness around the lake is a mecca for downhill and cross-country skiers in the winter.

I had come to Lake Tahoe thinking I would make a photograph without showing any of the commercial clutter, but wondered if that would be honest. I also wondered if I could show the lake in one or two photographs, or even fifty, given a subject that is twenty-two miles long, twelve miles wide, 1,645 feet deep, boasts more than seventy miles of shoreline, and has a big enough volume to drown all of California under fourteen inches of water.

The quickest route to the north side of Lake Tahoe is along California Highway 89, from the town of Truckee, which itself can be reached via the busy Interstate 80 freeway. I, however, exited Interstate 80 at the little community of Cisco, still some twenty miles or so from Truckee. I took Old Highway 40, the original route over the mountains, and part of the decommissioned U.S. Highway 40; the old route gave me a more convoluted and scenic entrance into Truckee.

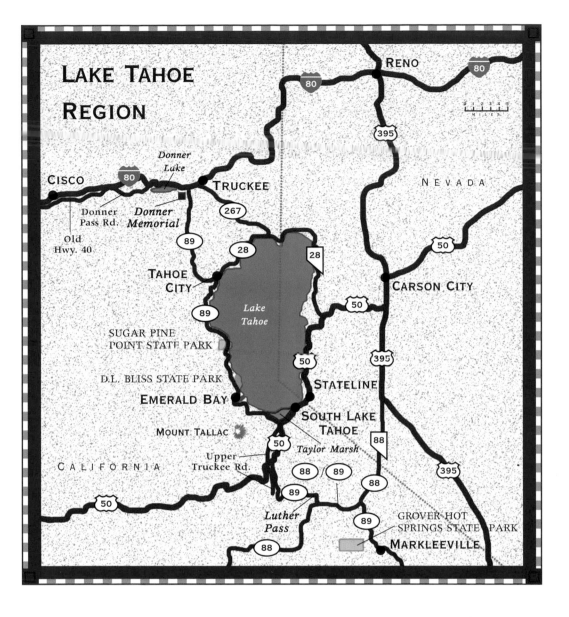

LAKE TAHOE REGION

CISCO
TRUCKEE
Donner Lake
Donner Pass Rd.
Donner Memorial
Old Hwy. 40
RENO
80
80
80
395
N E V A D A
267
89
28
28
89
TAHOE CITY
Lake Tahoe
50
CARSON CITY
SUGAR PINE POINT STATE PARK
89
50
D.L. BLISS STATE PARK
50
395
STATELINE
EMERALD BAY
SOUTH LAKE TAHOE
MOUNT TALLAC
Taylor Marsh
88
50
Upper Truckee Rd.
C A L I F O R N I A
88
89
88
395
89
50
89
GROVER HOT SPRINGS STATE PARK
Luther Pass
89
MARKLEEVILLE
88

About halfway to town, Old Highway 40 becomes Donner Pass Road. Just before it enters Truckee, Donner Pass Road leads by Donner Lake and the monument to the ill-fated Donner Party. Its members reached the Sierra Nevada Mountains in 1846, after winter snows closed the passes. Several people died and some of those that didn't had to resort to cannibalism.

Truckee used to be a logging, mining, and railroad town, but today it mostly serves tourists. Named for a Washoe Indian chief, Truckee's historic central business district, with its Old West storefronts and boardwalks, still exudes a frontier charm.

On my last trip to Lake Tahoe, I took

THE DONNER PARTY MEMORIAL, ON DONNER PASS ROAD, JUST OUTSIDE TRUCKEE.

California Highway 267 from Truckee, instead of the quicker Highway 89. Highway 267 climbs up Brockway Summit, offering panoramic views of the lake before making a steep descent through the forest to the Kings Beach and California Highway 28. Once I reached the lake, I turned right on Highway 28, heading counterclockwise around the northwest side of the lake. Several miles and too many stoplights later, I crossed the Truckee River, which flows out of the lake at Tahoe City.

Highway 28 ends at Tahoe City, which sits at the intersection with Highway 89. Highway 89 now travels along the western edge of the lake in one direction, and back to the town of Truckee in the other. During summer, the Truckee River, the only waterway to flow out of the lake, is dotted with rafters pulled along by the lazy current, while bicyclists, joggers, and in-line skaters parallel the river on a paved trail.

Emerald Bay

Heading south along the lake, the trappings of civilization are left behind as Highway 89 winds its way past the turnoff to the Homewood Ski Area and then through stands of Jeffrey and sugar pines. Two of the ten state parks around Lake Tahoe are near here, Sugar Pine Point and D. L. Bliss, offering opportunities to hike and camp. Then the highway climbs above Emerald Bay.

I pulled into the parking lot at the Eagle Falls viewpoint, and, five hundred feet below, I admired Emerald Bay, where the lake's clear water did reflect the deep blue color of the sky. The M. S. Dixie II, a paddle wheeler, was chugging around little Fannette Island, the only island on the lake. The bay, enormous in its own right, was dwarfed by the main body of Lake Tahoe.

I stayed for a while to enjoy the view and decided to pass on the mile walk down to the beach at Emerald Bay, where Vikingsholm Castle, a Scandinavian-style mansion built in 1929, sits in regal isolation. I turned to the west and looked above the opposite side of the highway at a portion of the Desolation Wilderness, which contains more than sixty-three thousand acres of forests, lakes, and granite peaks. Then I continued my drive around the lake, stopping briefly a few miles farther at the Inspiration Point overlook for another impressive view of Emerald Bay.

Taylor Marsh

Hoping I had the picture of Lake Tahoe that I needed, I drove down by the shoreline, stopping at the Forest Service Visitor Center adjacent to Taylor Marsh. I visited the Stream Profile Chamber, an underground viewing room where fish, including trout in spring and summer, and kokanee salmon in autumn, are diverted into a simulated stream environment. The Tallac Historic Site, on the other side of the parking lot from the visitor center, preserves several estates on the site of a resort area for the wealthy dating from the nineteenth century. The Camp Richardson Resort, still in operation and offering accommodations for every pocketbook, is just past Tallac.

I reached the city of South Lake Tahoe a few minutes after passing Camp Richardson. The hotels and casinos of the town of Stateline, on the Nevada side of the border, abut South Lake Tahoe. By chance, I met photographer Jon S. Paul in town, and he recommended a visit to Taylor Marsh itself. I decided to take his advice and visit the marsh the next day. That night, I slept under the stars at Fallen Leaf Campground, which is run by the Forest Service, one of thirty campgrounds around the lake. At dawn, all I had to do was climb out of my sleeping bag and brush my teeth before getting in my car. I drove a quarter mile, crossed Highway 89, and pulled into the parking lot for the marsh and the Tallac Resort.

I walked a few hundred yards out to the narrow beach dividing Taylor Marsh from Lake Tahoe. Mount Tallac, called "Great Mountain" by tribes that once lived in the region, was reflected in marsh ponds. I also walked along the Lake of the Sky Trail to a

CALIFORNIA SKETCH: AMELIA CELIO

The first Celio ranch house, built by pioneer Carlo Celio on Upper Truckee Road in the Upper Lake Valley in 1863, was replaced in 1914 by the tree-shaded home that still stands next to the old highway. Shirley Taylor, who lives in the old Celio house today and conducts the ranch's timber and cattle business, graciously shared some of the Celio family history with me.

Amelia Jelmini was born in 1871, and grew up to marry Frank Celio, Carlo's son. In some ways, Amelia Celio became the typical ranch wife who did the cooking and cleaning, as well as other, seemingly innumerable ranch chores. She liked to dance and enjoyed gardening. A master woodworker, Amelia made several pieces of furniture that are still in use in the ranch house.

But in a time and place when men usually conducted family business, Amelia Celio and her husband were equal partners in the enterprises that supplied much of South Lake Tahoe with lumber, beef, and dairy products. Amelia also participated in the annual cattle drives that moved the herd from the family's Lower Ranch, near Placerville, to summer pastures at Upper Ranch, and then back to Lower Ranch in the autumn. Amelia, who always wore a dress and boots during the cattle drives, would ride in a wagon for the five or six days it took to make the trips. Pregnant on her first October trip, she made the June 1902 drive in the company of her third child, Hazel Celio, who was two months old.

Most of the extensive pasture and timberlands once owned by the Celio family were sold long ago. Old Highway 89 is just a quiet backroad and Upper Lake Valley is now called Christmas Valley. History, however, has not been forgotten in the valley, where a plaque on the side of the road reads "The remaining property is being preserved as a tribute to the pioneering Celio family by a great granddaughter." That great granddaughter, Amelia's grandchild and the daughter of Hazel Celio, is Shirley Taylor.

ABOVE:

AMELIA CELIO, CIRCA 1890. (COURTESY OF SHIRLEY TAYLOR.)

---

viewing deck that projected out into the marsh. Although I didn't see any bald eagles, which roost in the marsh during the winter, I did observe a beaver swimming in one of the ponds, along with ducks and geese.

The lake itself was covered in a mist that began to rise as sunlight touched the water. Back at the beach I photographed a gaggle of Canada geese swim close to shore. I shivered a little, not from the cold, but from excitement, because I knew the geese, the mist, and the morning light gave me the photograph I wanted of the noble sheet of blue water.

The Upper Truckee Road

The Upper Truckee Road is a quiet, historic alternative to Highway 89. It begins where Highway 89 and U.S. Highway 50 first meet, just south of Lake Tahoe. After ten miles and a series of steep switchbacks, the old road ends back at Highway 89, a few miles shy of Luther Pass and the southern end of the Tahoe Basin.

To reach this road, which includes part of the original Highway 89, first turn right from Emerald Bay Road (Highway 89) at the Y intersection in South Lake Tahoe onto Lake Tahoe Boulevard. Two miles farther up the road, Lake Tahoe Boulevard becomes North Upper Truckee Road and winds past several tree-shaded housing tracts.

After crossing U.S. 50, the route becomes South Upper Truckee Road which is, in fact, the original Highway 89, running through what was once called Upper Lake Valley. About a mile south of U.S. 50, the road reaches a roadside plaque marking the site of the historic Celio Ranch. Another four miles brings you back to a short set of switchbacks and a small cascade, just before reaching the junction with the present Highway 89.

Luther Pass to Markleeville

Beyond the intersection with South Upper Truckee Road, Highway 89 climbs through steep, forested slopes to reach Luther Pass, 7,740 feet above sea level. Beyond the pass, the highway enters Alpine County and the scenic Hope Valley with its spacious meadows surrounded by many tall peaks.

Most of Hope Valley is owned by the California Department of Fish and Game. The land, once owned by ranchers in Nevada who let their cattle roam the meadows during the summer, is now protected as a wildlife refuge and is closed to motorized traffic.

The cattle and the cowboys are gone. Now, the ruins of an old homestead stand just inside the boundary of the state-owned property, where Highway 89 comes close to the floor of the valley. Park your car, walk to the homestead, and survey, as the owners once did, the beautiful valley and the sur-

rounding peaks.

The West Fork of the Carson River flows through Hope Valley, and Highway 89 crosses it just before intersecting with California Highway 88. To the east, the two highways share one road for a few miles, passing the Kit Carson Forest Service campground and Woodfords, a former pony express stop where a country store now stands. While Highway 88 continues east to U.S. 395 and the Nevada border, Highway 89 jogs right at Woodfords, and continues south about six miles to the picturesque village of Markleeville, the Alpine County seat. Grover Hot Springs State Park, with commercial pools and a campground, is about three miles west of Markleeville.

Markleeville

Markleeville, with a main street just a few blocks long, is named for Jacob Marklee, who built a cabin at Markleeville Creek in

HOPE VALLEY AND THE HIGH SIERRA PEAKS OF ALPINE COUNTY, ALONG HIGHWAY 89 ON THE SOUTH SIDE OF LUTHER PASS.

1861. A few years before Marklee's arrival, silver had been discovered near the headwaters of the Carson River, where the now vanished town of Silver Mountain City sprang up, a few miles from Markleeville. Marklee built a toll bridge to span the middle fork of the Carson River, and the community which grew up around the bridge came to be known as Markleeville. Alpine County, with its bounty of high peaks, was created in 1864, and, at that time, had a population of more than eleven thousand. When the silver played out, people began to leave the county, although Markleeville continued to serve as a supply center for ranchers and loggers. Today, Alpine County has the smallest population of any county in the state. The 150 residents of Markleeville make up a tenth of the county's population, and the town tends largely to the needs of tourists.

Many of Markleeville's buildings are made of wood. Several old buildings from town were moved a few blocks and are preserved at the Alpine County Museum, which sits on a knoll and offers a commanding view of Markleeville and the High Sierra peaks.

The three-story Alpine Hotel, located in the middle of town, is another building of wood construction, with an unusual history. It was known as the Fisk Hotel when it was constructed in 1862, not in Markleeville, but in Silver Mountain City. Markleeville suf-

fered a serious fire in 1885 and lost its own hotel. The Fisk was dismantled board by board and was reassembled in Markleeville in 1886 as the Hot Springs Hotel, and today is known as the Alpine Hotel.

The Cutthroat Saloon, located in the hotel, deserves at least one visit. A written description of the Cutthroat would not do it justice. In this case, a picture is worth a thousand words.

YOSEMITE NATIONAL PARK

The earliest memories I have are of Yosemite. I can recall my father holding me in his arms, turning around slowly to show me Yosemite Falls and the towering granite walls of Yosemite Valley. I've been back to Yosemite more times than I can count, and I've seen many other parents hold their own children to show them Yosemite, as my father did so long ago.

It's difficult to write about Yosemite without slipping into clichés, but perhaps naturalist John Muir summed up the feelings many people have instinctively about the park when he wrote, "No temple made with hands can compare with Yosemite."

Like my parents, most people who visit Yosemite spend most of their time in the valley, which is just seven miles square and can be explored by car in less than an hour. That includes a recommended lunch at Degnan's Deli in Yosemite Village, although time spent looking for a parking space doesn't count.

But don't be tempted to rush through Yosemite. If you are, remember the story about the visitor who asked an old ranger what he should do for the hour he had in the park. "Son," the ranger said, "if I only had an hour I'd sit by the river and cry."

There is good reason to visit Yosemite Valley, since it contains many of the park's most famous natural wonders. Yosemite Falls, which plunges 2,425 feet from the rim of the valley to its floor, is the highest waterfall in North America and the fifth tallest in the world, while El Capitan is the single

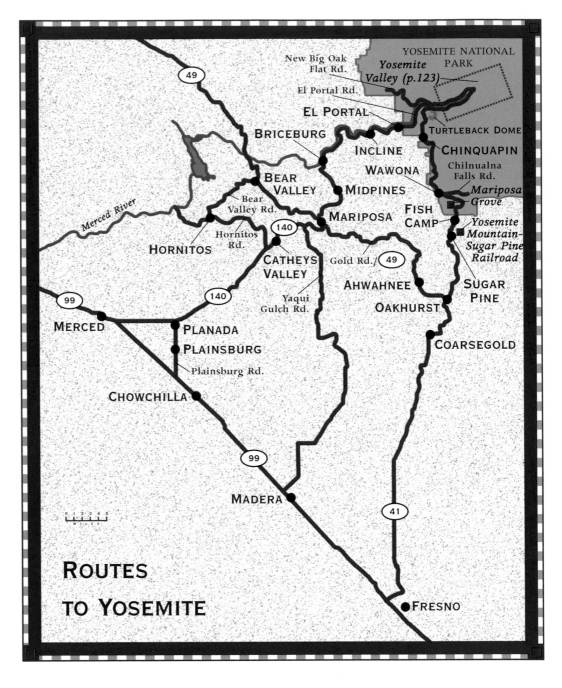

ROUTES TO YOSEMITE

largest granite rock on earth. Half Dome, the Valley's towering backdrop, was split by glaciers that began to flow through the park sixty thousand years ago. Indeed, the sites in the valley are extraordinary.

But during the summer, when the valley becomes crowded with visitors, cars, and tour buses, it's a good idea to spend some time in the other 1,163 square miles of the park, including high country peaks, alpine lakes, groves of giant sequoia trees, historic buildings, and deep river canyons that boast

their own cascades and waterfalls.

The routes described in these pages include some of the park's 196 miles of paved roads. But be forewarned. As John Muir wrote in 1890, the journey to Yosemite can be "a long one; not because of the miles, for they are not so many—only about 250 from San Francisco, and passed over by rail and carriage roads in a day or two—but the way is so beautiful that one is beguiled at every step, and the great golden days and weeks and months go by uncounted."

Fresno to Wawona

The community of Wawona is a little over four thousand feet in elevation, and is within Yosemite about five miles beyond the southern entrance. Originally called Clark's Station, after Yosemite pioneer Galen Clark, Wawona was a stagecoach stop on the way to the valley. Today, most people who enter Wawona on California Highway 41 simply continue to the valley, still some twenty miles away. But Wawona has a significant number of attractions that make it a worthy destination in its own right.

To reach Wawona, take Highway 41 north from the Central Valley city of Fresno. At first the highway stays reasonably flat, leaving behind the northward bulge of commercial buildings and new housing developments before it reaches open country. Then the road swings east and begins to climb into the Sierra Nevada foothills, the landscape studded with boulders and oaks. As the highway continues to climb, the oaks begin to share the scenery with pines.

About forty miles north of Fresno, Highway 41 reaches the little community of Coarsegold, where a solid gold nugget worth fifteen thousand dollars (in 1849 dollars) was found during the gold rush. Beyond Coarsegold, the road rises steeply to crest a ridge. On the far side of the ridge the road drops down into a wide valley and the town of Oakhurst.

Originally called Fresno Flats, Oakhurst offers visitors all the amenities the modern traveler needs and has become something of a fast food emporium. Blame—or praise—the rise of fast food in Oakhurst on the growing number of tourists who pass through town and who must be fed, and on a permanent population that has grown steadily over the past few decades, a population augmented by retirees, many who have escaped from Los Angeles.

Historic California Highway 49 (the Gold Road) reaches its southern terminus at Oakhurst. Taking the Gold Road north five miles leads to the little community of Ahwahnee, and the Wassama Round House, a ceremonial lodge on state parkland, which is still used by the Miwok. The town of Mariposa lies another twenty miles past Ahwahnee.

Our route to Wawona, however, continues north along Highway 41. The road climbs out of the valley and crosses the Lewis Fork of the Fresno River before pass-

ing a Sierra National Forest ranger station. This is a good place to stop and obtain maps and information about the national forest lands around Yosemite.

As the highway contours around the southern slopes of the foothills, the oaks begin to give way to pines and cedars and dogwood. By the time the road reaches four thousand feet, the oaks have disappeared altogether, and the foothills have turned into mountains. About ten miles beyond Oakhurst, the road reaches the Yosemite Mountain–Sugar Pine Railroad, which hauled lumber from 1899 to 1931. Presently from mid-April through October, the railroad ferries tourists in old logging cars on a forty-five–minute ride into Lewis Creek Canyon.

A few miles beyond the railroad, the highway reaches the little town of Fish Camp, home of Tenaya Lodge. While offering deluxe accommodations for the nearby national park, the enormous hotel is out of character with its more humble surroundings. Mercifully, the Marriott Corporation built the lodge almost completely out of sight from the highway.

The highway passes a national forest "snow play" area—popular with families who like to slide downhill on their sleds in winter—and then enters Yosemite National Park. Just beyond the entrance station, a right turn leads two miles to the Mariposa Grove of giant sequoia trees. During winter, the road to the grove is apt to be closed, though it can be reached by hardy visitors on skis or snowshoes. From late spring through early autumn, the grove can be explored by tram or on foot. A one-mile loop trail leads to the Grizzly Giant, the largest sequoia in the grove and the fifth largest sequoia in the world. Park naturalists believe the tree is more than twenty-seven hundred years old.

Returning to our journey toward Yosemite Valley, Highway 41 skirts a meadow as it enters Wawona. The eastern half of the meadow, where horses once grazed, is now a nine-hole golf course. On the right side of

the road, the elegant, Victorian-era Wawona Hotel sits back from the highway on manicured lawns. The original Wawona Hotel, built by Galen Clark, was about a mile away. The new hotel replaced Clark's less formal accommodations, and was situated closer to the highway.

With its quaint dining room—the lampshades feature forest scenes—and comfortable sitting rooms, several tennis courts, a swimming pool, and the golf course, the Wawona Hotel makes for a very pleasant stay. I've been fortunate enough to spend a few nights at the hotel. It's not, however, the only place to spend time in Wawona.

Just around the corner from Wawona's grocery store and gas station, on Chilnualna Falls Road, there is a clutch of privately owned homes within the park boundary. The land on which these homes sit, known as Section 35 by the Park Service, was originally part of the Sierra National Forest and was incorporated into the national park in the 1930s. The people who owned homes in Wawona were allowed to stay, and today there are a few hundred houses on the site. Some of these dwellings are best described as rustic, others as deluxe. Many of these private residences can be rented for vacation stays through a private company, and I have a few favorites I've stayed in over the years. Set back about a mile from Highway 41, these homes are out of sight and unknown to most park visitors.

The road running past the homes ends at Lower Chilnualna Fall, about two miles off of Highway 41. This impressive cascade courses with wild abandon in spring and early summer. Upper Chilnualna Fall can be reached from a trailhead and parking lot near the lower falls.

Wawona holds at least two other attractions. One is the Wawona Campground. Used by the U.S. Army from 1891 to 1906, as a base of operations before there were park rangers to protect the park. The campground's one hundred sites are open throughout the year. The campground lies in a narrow strip of forested land, with the

South Fork of the Merced River on one side and Highway 41 on the other.

The other attraction is the Pioneer Yosemite History Center, just around the corner from the hotel, where there are several historic buildings and cabins, including a schoolhouse, blacksmith shop, and jail, as well as a number of restored wagons and a stagecoach. Almost all the buildings at the center have been moved from other parts of Yosemite. However, the covered bridge, built in 1858, spans the South Fork of the Merced River at its original site. During the summer, docents dressed in period costumes assume the role of soldiers, teachers, and pioneers who lived a century or more ago. Don't, by the way, attempt to bring up current events with these somewhat ethereal residents of Yosemite. A question about politics put to a U.S. cavalryman, for example, is apt to bring a reply about President Lincoln.

Wawona to the Yosemite Valley

Once past Wawona, Highway 41 begins a relentless, two-thousand-foot climb over nine miles, contouring steep slopes and crossing several creeks. Although there are some wonderful views of the Central Valley, much of the route travels through deep forest.

The highway passes by the turnoff to Yosemite West, a collection of homes just outside the national park, which can only be reached by driving into the park on Highway 41. A little past Yosemite West the road reaches Chinquapin, named for the evergreen shrub found in profusion here. Chinquapin is also the turnoff to a dead-end road to spectacular Glacier Point, sixteen miles distant, which overlooks Yosemite Valley and the high country beyond. This is also the route to the Badger Pass Ski Area during the winter, when the Glacier Point Road is open for only the first six miles, just far enough to reach the ski hills.

Once past Chinquapin, the highway begins to drop toward Yosemite Valley. Along this stretch of Highway 41, there are views into the Merced River Canyon and of the devastation caused by the massive 1989 fires.

Six miles after leaving Chinquapin, the road crosses the granitic, and aptly named Turtleback Dome. Some granite domes, like Half Dome, are enormous. They can be found from Lake Tahoe in the northern Sierra to the southern end of the range, although they exist in their grandest profusion in Yosemite. The domes, which were originally molten magma that cooled to become granite lying beneath the earth, were formed when gla-

CALIFORNIA SKETCH: GALEN CLARK

Galen Clark was laid to rest almost a century ago, beneath the four giant sequoias he planted himself well in anticipation of his death. Clark, who entered Yosemite as one of its first tourists, would also become one of the park's most celebrated residents, eclipsed in fame only by John Muir and Ansel Adams. His efforts to promote and preserve Yosemite have not been forgotten, but much of his curious, personal history is not well known.

Clark was born on the farm his parents carved out of the Canadian wilderness. When he was five, his family, unable to cope with the rough demands of the far north, moved to a small community in New Hampshire. Clark claimed late in his life that he was placed in a home with friends of his family, living apart from his parents and siblings until he was seventeen. The claimed abandonment, however, has never been corroborated.

As Clark grew to adulthood, he realized he really wasn't happy farming in the harsh climate of New England, in part because he apparently suffered lung problems. Moving away from the farm as a young man, he was apprenticed as a house painter and furniture maker. Later, he tried his hand in business but failed in several ventures.

His wife, Rebecca, died in Philadelphia in 1848, and Clark left his five children to the care of relatives, just as he claimed his own parents had left him. He traveled to California, lured by the gold rush and the mild weather, but he found work in the goldfields to be unrewarding. Soon, he went to work for John C. Fremont, who wanted to bring water from the South Fork of the Merced River to his dry diggings near Mariposa. Clark served as a horse packer, surveyor, and camp manager.

Not long after, Yosemite's natural wonders were publicized by James Hutchings, a British miner who became a journalist and early booster of Yosemite's commercial possibilities. There were no roads or even horse trails when the first tourists to Yosemite, Clark among them, made their way into the Yosemite Valley in 1855. Two enterprising brothers, Milton and Houston Mann, decided to build a toll road from the South Fork of the Merced River into the Yosemite Valley, starting at the present day site of Wawona. Like Clark, the Mann brothers were among the first tourists to Yosemite, and like Hutchings, they correctly anticipated that many more people would soon follow them.

Galen Clark was forty-two years old. After his lungs began to hemorrhage in the goldfields, he suspected his death was imminent. He later wrote that at the time he was "given up to die at any hour. . . . I went to the mountains to take my chances of dying or growing better which I thought were about even." Clark, despite his stated aversion to farming and physical labor, began to recreate himself in the crucible of wilderness, succeeding where his parents, on their Canadian homestead, had failed.

He built a cabin near the start of the Mann brothers' toll road in 1857, where the river and the lush meadows provided water and good grazing for the tourist's tired horses. The Indians were friendly with Clark, and they called his first, rude abode *Pallahchun*, "A Good Place to Stay." Soon he took over the role as an informal innkeeper at "Clark's Station" for the growing number of tourists on their way to Yosemite Valley. At first Clark charged a nominal amount for those he fed and put up for a night, or sometimes charged nothing at all. Over time Clark's Station was enlarged and improved, and Clark was joined by a partner, but the hotel didn't make Clark a wealthy man. He eventually sold the hotel to pay off debts.

Clark was one of the first white men to view the giant sequoias in the Mariposa Grove, naming the grove in honor of the county in which the trees grew. The Nuchu word for the big trees was wa-wo-na, and Clark so called the land around his cabin Wawona. Clark began guiding visitors to the Mariposa Grove as well as into the valley, and he advocated protecting both Yosemite Valley and the Mariposa Grove from commercial development.

President Lincoln directed that Yosemite Valley and the Mariposa Grove be administered by the state of California as a park, and Clark was appointed its first official guardian, or resident superintendent. (Yosemite National Park, surrounding the Valley, was created after the Yosemite Valley and Mariposa Grove grant, and the three areas were not integrated into one unit for several years.) Clark was reappointed to the same position some years later, and he continued to champion the preservation of Yosemite's natural treasures. Clark often locked horns with James Hutchings until the latter's death in an accident on Big Oak Flat Road just outside the valley.

Clark's knowledge about Yosemite, his collection of books about philosophy and the natural world, his ability to climb mountains and mediate disputes between concessionaires, and his poetry writing and his hospitality to tourists made him a living legend. He was equally at ease with miners and intellectuals, such as Ralph Waldo Emerson and Horace Greeley, who came to see the wonders of Yosemite. Clark was particularly friendly with the naturalist John Muir, who was instrumental in enlarging the park boundaries and helped found the Sierra Club. Later in life, Clark became reacquainted with two of his three surviving children.

Clark came to Yosemite not knowing if he would survive a single year in the wilderness. The mountains must have effected the cure he sought, for he managed to live more than long enough to enter the pantheon of Yosemite's heroes. Clark, in fact, lived fifty-four years after building his little cabin at Wawona, his suspect lungs not betraying him until the age of ninety-six. His remains, in the gravesite he chose for himself years earlier, are in the Pioneer Cemetery in Yosemite Valley, under the shade of those four sequoias.

GALEN CLARK AT THE BASE OF A GIANT REDWOOD, CIRCA 1859. (PHOTOGRAPH BY CARLETON WATKINS. COURTESY OF YOSEMITE NATIONAL PARK.)

ABOVE:
LOOKING OUT OVER THE YOSEMITE VALLEY FROM TUNNEL VIEW, WITH FAMED EL CAPITAN ON THE LEFT AND HALF DOME IN THE BACKGROUND.

RIGHT:
AN ARTISTIC RENDITION OF YOSEMITE FALLS ON A MID-MORNING IN SPRING.

ciers removed the older, overlying rock. The release of pressure on the granite allowed layers of rock to peel away in shells, in a process called exfoliation.

A pullout on the canyon side of the highway offers a fantastic preview of wonders to come, with El Capitan and Half Dome clearly visible to the east. During spring and early summer, Cascade Creek, across the canyon, crosses New Big Oak Flat Road and roars down the mountain to join the Merced River.

Just beyond the pullout, the road enters the nearly mile long Wawona Tunnel, which was blasted through the granite to provide a shorter, easier route than the original toll road that climbed over the mountain the tunnel now bores through.

Tunnel View, the classic viewpoint of Yosemite Valley, lies just beyond the far end of the tunnel. The flat, heavily forested valley floor was scooped out by glaciers millennia ago. The valley is surrounded by colossal cliffs of granite, including the mighty Half Dome and Clouds Rest Peak soaring in the background. El Capitan, its sheer granite face a magnet for rock climbers seeking the ultimate mountaineering experience, looms on the north side of the valley. On the south, Bridalveil Fall plunges 620 feet, between the Cathedral Spires and the Leaning Tower.

Parking lots at Tunnel View are on either side of the road, and they are apt to be crowded during the summer months. Even finding elbow room to make a photograph can be a chore.

From the Wawona Tunnel, the road plunges one-and-a-half steep miles to the Yosemite Valley floor, reaching the entrance to the Bridalveil Fall parking lot. Although a short trail leads to the base of the falls, the parking lot provides the best view. On clear days in the latter half of October, watch for a rainbow to develop at the base of the falls at 4:30 P.M. As the sun, invisible behind granite walls, reaches a position that is 180 degrees opposite Bridalveil, the rainbow will slowly travel from the bottom to the top of the waterfall.

In autumn, Bridalveil Fall especially lives up to its name. The reduced flow of water, blowing back and forth in even a light wind across the granite walls over which it descends, looks like a translucent veil. In the spring, the waterfall literally leaps off the rim of the cliff and pours as if from a gargantuan water faucet onto the valley floor and into the Merced River.

Southside Drive

Past Bridalveil, the one-way Southside Drive heads east, toward the top of the valley, before looping back as Northside Drive. There are pullouts and picnic areas all along the way. The road passes Leidig Meadow, and there is a first good look at Yosemite Falls. Leaping free of the rim, Yosemite Falls drops 2,425 feet over the granite cliff to the valley floor. The Upper Fall alone is only slightly shorter than Chicago's Sears Tower, and the Lower Fall is nearly twice the height of Niagara Falls.

Sentinel Bridge, just across the road from the Yosemite Chapel, beckons photographers almost every sunset. The road over the bridge leads to Yosemite Village and Yosemite Lodge. Northside Drive, however, continues east, past the bridge, following the upstream course of the Merced River to Curry Village, where there are more accommodations and shops. Granite walls rise almost four thousand feet directly behind and above Curry Village to Glacier Point. Foot and bike trails plus free shuttle busses travel to Happy Isles, where there is a nature center. A supersonic blast of air, triggered by a massive rock slide, blew down many trees at Happy Isles in the summer of 1996. More trees were swept away by the 1997 flood. The effects of these natural events are apparent in the treeless landscape.

The road, now with traffic running in both directions, continues past Curry Village and Stoneman Meadow, the latter offering grand views of Half Dome and North Dome on either side of the valley. Two campgrounds lie beyond the meadow, as do stables, where visitors can begin a horseback ride through the valley or up trails along the granite walls to Vernal and Nevada Falls. Cars are not allowed past the stables, although hikers and bikers can continue on pavement to Mirror Lake, now almost filled with enough sediment to make it a meadow.

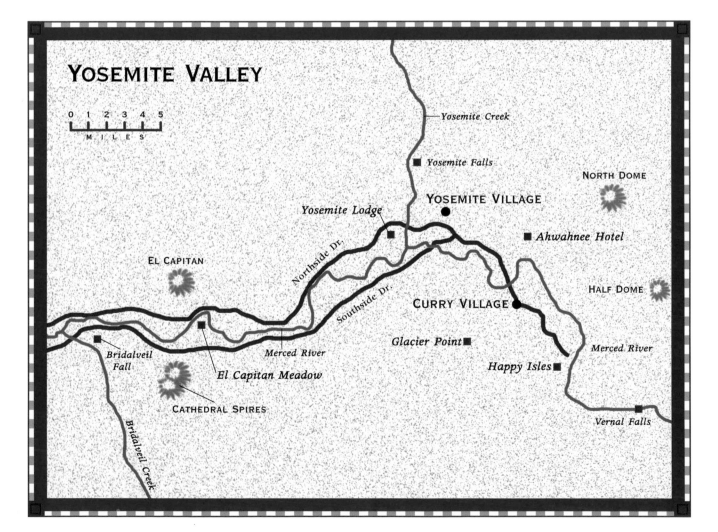

Apple orchards planted by pioneers behind the stables attract bears when the fruit ripens in summer and autumn.

Northside Drive

Backtracking to Curry Village, a right turn leads north for a quarter mile onto another one-way road and heads over Stoneman Bridge. Beyond the campgrounds the road bends west onto Northside Drive, leading past a meadow boarded on one end by the pleasant homes of the park's concessionaires, who enjoy a magnificent view of Half Dome. Watch for unusual pink dogwood that blooms in front of one of the houses in early May.

The road continues past the meadow to the turnoff to Yosemite Village, a chokepoint for cars during the summer and on any weekend from spring through autumn. The visitor center and Ansel Adams Gallery are just past the Village Store, as is the little-visited Pioneer Cemetery and the replica of a Maidu village, which contains an authentic ceremonial round house. This is also the way to the famed Ahwahnee Hotel.

The hotel opened July 14, 1927, cost a then staggering $1.8 million, and went a million dollars over budget. Its opening, designed to coincide with the opening of the All Year Highway (California Highway 140 from Merced to the Yosemite Valley), was months behind schedule. Some of the one thousand tons of steel and five thousand tons of rock used to build the Ahwahnee were hauled up the new highway.

With mighty Half Dome serving as a backdrop, the massive, six-story hotel, with its three wings, sits at the edge of the Ahwahnee Meadow. On the ground floor, cathedral-like ceilings, twenty-three–foot high windows topped with stained glass, and promethean-sized stone hearths compete for attention with collections of Native American and Oriental rugs, wall murals, Miwok Indian baskets, and historical photographs.

The hotel was designed to appeal to the wealthy, and today's prices for rooms are

certainly not inexpensive. Despite the cost, the hotel is often booked solid more than a year in advance. But guests and visitors alike can relax for free in the Great Lounge, sit outside on the patio, and enjoy reasonably priced meals—given the surroundings—in the main dining room.

The Bracebridge Dinner, a Christmas pageant, takes place in the dining room on December 22, Christmas Eve, and Christmas Day. Based on sketches created by Washington Irving, who wrote the famed *Rip Van Winkle* and *The Legend of Sleepy Hollow* tales, and adapted by Yosemite photographer Ansel Adams, the pageant includes an elaborate dinner, classic carols, Renaissance rituals, and medieval music.

Don't imagine you can just drop in for the pageant, however. A yearly lottery for the 1,675 seats available for each of the three Bracebridge Dinners garners requests from 60,000 would-be diners.

Northside Drive continues past the hotel and becomes a two-way road again. Watch on the right during spring for what appear to be dogwood blossoms, though they are in fact apple blossoms. They grow on trees planted by pioneers, and you can come back in autumn when the apples are ripe and take a bite of history.

Just over the bridge spanning Yosemite Creek on the right side of the road, is the Yosemite Falls parking lot. A trail leads a little over a quarter of a mile to the foot of the Lower Fall.

ABOVE:
A MULE DEER GRAZES IN THE BACKLIT GRASS OF COOKS MEADOW IN YOSEMITE VALLEY.

FACING PAGE:
HALF DOME FRAMED BY AUTUMNAL OAK LEAVES.

ABOVE, LEFT:
THE INTERIOR OF A
ROUND HOUSE SHOWN
IN THE REPLICA OF A
MAIDU VILLAGE NEXT TO
THE VISITOR CENTER.

ABOVE, RIGHT:
SNOW MANTLES THE
AHWAHNEE HOTEL AND
THE GRANITE CLIFFS
BEHIND IT ON NEW
YEAR'S DAY.

The entrance to Yosemite Lodge is opposite the falls parking lot. A few hundred rustic cabins that had stood on the lodge's grounds were seriously damaged by the 1997 flood and were torn down late in 1998. Since they were in the Merced River floodplain, the Park Service does not intend to replace them. More modern motel facilities remain at the lodge, and cabins are still available at Curry Village.

Just past the lodge the road comes to the vacant site of a gas station, which was also removed after the flood. The adjacent Sunnyside Campground, called Camp Four by Yosemite's rock climbers, remains intact and available on a first-come, first-served basis.

Northside Drive, now a one-way road yet again, continues west along the course of the serpentine Merced River to reach El Capitan Meadow. Park on either side of the road and, from spring through autumn, join the crowds looking for climbers on the granite face of El Capitan. Don't forget to turn around and look at Cathedral Spires, made up of an almost surreal collection of pinnacles and cliffs. Watch particularly on the left-hand ridge of massive Middle Cathedral, where climbers can often be spotted against the granite pillar.

Except in winter, there are apt to be many parties of climbers attempting to scale El Capitan. Although the climb has been done in a day, most people take several days, and the first successful ascent took place over two summers! Boyfriends, girlfriends, and spouses of the climbers often sit in El Capitan Meadow, watching the progress of their loved ones through binoculars and spotting scopes.

Back on Northside Drive, watch as the road crosses over a ridge of rocky rubble. It's the western edge of the snout of the last glacier to flow through the Yosemite Valley, between twenty thousand and sixty thousand years ago. The line of debris that accumulates in front of the snout is called the terminal glacial moraine. Bridalveil Fall comes into view on the left, a little less than two miles past El Capitan Meadow. This is also a good place to see how much of the bank of the Merced River was torn away by the floodwaters in 1997. A pullout is just beyond the damaged riverbank, offering a final, picture-perfect view of the valley, with El Capitan on the left and Bridalveil Fall and Cathedral Spires on the right.

A few hundred yards past the pullout, Northside Drive ends at the beginning of El Portal Road, commonly referred to in Yosemite as Highway 41. If you turn left at the stop sign onto El Portal Road and travel a few yards, you will find Fern Spring beneath a canopy of dogwood on the right side of the road. Whimsically referred to as Yosemite's smallest waterfall, the spring is about a foot high. It's also home to the rare lungwort, a plant that requires constant shade and moisture. Both requirements are in good supply at Fern Spring, which offers a charming counterpoint to the larger, more famous waterfalls of Yosemite Valley.

Beyond Fern Spring, El Portal Road loops east and splits near Bridalveil Fall, leading onto Southside Drive, or back to Wawona.

Instead of turning left from Northside Drive at the stop sign, you can continue west onto El Portal Road, which is identified by a sign just before the junction as Highway 140. El Portal Road leads down into the Merced River Gorge and the Merced River Canyon to El Portal and, ultimately, the Central Valley. About a mile past the Northside Drive/El Portal Road junction, on El Portal Road, you will reach the junction with New Big Oak Flat Road, which leads north to California Highway 120 toward Tioga Pass and Tuolumne Meadows, in the Yosemite high country.

Merced to Mariposa

The Highway 140 byway runs through largely undeveloped country, traveling from the pleasant Central Valley city of Merced to the former gold rush community of Mari-

posa. It's also the route of choice for many visitors traveling to Yosemite Valley in the winter, since Highway 140 is usually the last road into the park to be affected by snow.

Merced is a little over one hundred miles east of San Francisco and about three hundred miles north of Los Angeles. Highway 140 travels due east from the center of Merced for the first five miles or so, to the farming community of Tuttle, and continues another few miles to Planada.

Those traveling from the south of Merced can take the Planada shortcut to Highway 140. It's the route I take when I come from my home in Los Angeles on my way to Mariposa or Yosemite in winter. To take the shortcut, which is off of California Highway 99, drive about five miles north of the town of Chowchilla and take the Plainsburg Road

A WALNUT GROVE ALONG PLAINSBURG ROAD, WHICH OFFERS A SHORTCUT FROM HIGHWAY 99 SOUTH OF MERCED TO THE FARMING COMMUNITY OF PLANADA ON HIGHWAY 140.

exit. There are a few stop signs on this two-lane road, but it's a straight shot to Highway 140, mostly through groves of walnut trees. After the first few miles, the road passes through the community of Plainsburg, where there are no services, before reaching Planada, where there is a market and gas station, and where a housing development on the south side of town is closing in on the walnut groves and open pastureland. Once Highway 140 is reached, turn right.

About five miles farther, the highway reaches the boundary between Merced and Mariposa counties. Mariposa County was one of the original counties created when California became a state in 1850. Called the

OWL'S CLOVER AND LUPINE ALONG YAQUI GULCH ROAD.

"Mother of the Counties," Mariposa spanned the Central Valley from the Coast Ranges to the Nevada state line and reached all the way to Los Angeles County in the south. It comprised some 30,000 square miles, about one-fifth of California. Six new counties were eventually carved out of Mariposa County and five surrounding counties received added portions of Mariposa County. Now Mariposa contains a mere 1,455 square miles.

The walnut groves fade away into seemingly endless acres of open pastureland. For the next few miles the road begins a gentle climb into the Sierra Nevada foothills. As the roadbed steepens, watch for bright orange algae on some of the boulders in the adjacent fields.

The turnoff onto Hornitos Road, leading to the once bustling town of Hornitos, is about twenty-four miles east of Merced, and makes for a good side trip. Now a small town, Hornitos lies about twelve miles to the north along winding roads and has several old buildings, including St. Catherine's Church, which dates to the 1860s.

At the north end of town, Bear Valley Road (County Road J16) heads north and then east out of Hornitos, and travels through ranchland before switchbacking six miles up through thick groves of oak trees, to rendezvous with Highway 49. The town of Mariposa lies a few miles south.

If you skip the trip to Hornitos, you'll find Highway 140 gradually climbs through a series of low, round hills and drops down into Catheys Valley, which was settled by a pioneer family during the gold rush. The picturesque valley is dotted with old ranch houses, barns, and oak trees. One unusual stop is the Chibchas restaurant and inn, which has featured Colombian cuisine for over thirty years.

Beyond Catheys Valley, the highway reaches Yaqui Gulch Road, which connects with a few other roads to offer a scenic backroads route to the Central Valley town of Madera and Highway 99, thirty miles south of Merced.

Mariposa

Highway 140 reaches the town of Mariposa a few miles past Yaqui Gulch Road. Once a bustling gold rush town, Mariposa today is a quiet community from late autumn through early spring. But Mariposa enjoys another kind of gold rush fever during the summer months, when tourists flock through town on their way to Yosemite.

The southern end of Mariposa contains a few picturesque blocks of storefront buildings, and there are several more historic structures scattered throughout the town, including California's oldest courthouse, built in 1854 and still in use; the courthouse is on Ninth and Bullion Streets, just east of Highway 140 and downtown Mariposa. The town also contains the Mariposa County History Center, with gold-mining and Miwok cultural displays, as well as an extensive library of historical documents. The California State Mining and Mineral Museum, on Highway 140 just north of downtown, features a collection of gold nuggets.

The newer part of town is to the north, along Highway 140, where aficionados of hamburgers and milk shakes will want to pay a visit to the Happy Burger restaurant, a throwback to 1950s diners with more than two hundred items on the menu. I can attest to the burgers, fries, salads, and ice cream cones—all are lip-smacking good.

The members of the 1806 Gabriel Moraga expedition were unable to find their way to Happy Burger, but they did find *mariposas* (Spanish for "butterflies"), in profusion along a stream in the Sierra Nevada foothills, and so named the place and the land around it Mariposa.

The town, or more properly, the mining camp of Mariposa, sprang up after gold was discovered early in 1849. Rich deposits of surface gold drew miners from surrounding areas, and gold-bearing quartz veins were discovered later, which meant that Mariposa would remain an important mining center for several years.

The land on which Mariposa was founded belonged to John C. Fremont, who, as mentioned earlier, explored the Great Basin and California. Fremont was also instrumental in gaining California's independence from Mexico. Fremont had obtained more than forty thousand acres, known as the Las Mariposas Land Grant. It was a "floating grant," its precise boundaries not set at the time Fremont obtained it. Fremont prevailed in the ensuing legal battles over the mining rights.

Fremont and his wife never lived in Mariposa, but they did have a home in nearby Bear Valley, north along Highway 49.

ABOVE:
A BARN IN CATHEYS VALLEY, ALONG HIGHWAY 140.

LEFT:
BEAR VALLEY ROAD, NEAR THE TOWN OF HORNITOS, WIGGLES ITS WAY INTO THE SIERRA NEVADA FOOTHILLS, TO RENDEZVOUS WITH HIGHWAY 49.

Mariposa to El Portal

Highway 140, originally known as the All Year Highway, is rarely touched by the winter snows. Construction of the highway began early in the twentieth century, and the route was designed to take travelers from the Central Valley into Yosemite National Park when other mountain roads were closed. Even though snow can sometimes fall at elevations as low as one thousand feet, Highway 140 rarely closes, though tire chains should always be carried during winter months.

Before reaching its spectacular climax in the Merced River Canyon, Highway 140 heads north from Mariposa for two miles. The road reaches its highest point, almost three thousand feet in elevation, at the community of Midpines, where there is a little country market and a few nearby motels. Past Midpines the road makes a precipitous drop through the Bear Creek Canyon on the Briceburg Grade, heading to a rendezvous with the Merced River fifteen hundred feet below.

The Briceburg Bridge at the community of Briceburg crosses *El Rio Nuestra Señora de la Merced*, The River of Our Lady of Mercy, known today simply as the Merced River. It was originally named by the Spanish explorer Gabriel Moraga in 1806—the same Moraga who named Mariposa. The narrow, steep canyon provides a magnificent setting for the river, which begins life well to the east in the High Sierra of Yosemite National Park.

Highway 140 stays on the south side of the river, turning east to follow it upstream toward the community of El Portal and Yosemite. The Briceburg Bridge, constructed in 1937 by the U.S. Forest Service, leads to a dirt road on the north side of the river. This is the abandoned right of way of the Yosemite Valley Railroad, which connected Merced and El Portal from 1907 until 1945. At El Portal, passengers would board a stagecoach for the final ride into the Yosemite Valley.

The railroad struggled after the All Year Highway was completed in the mid-1920s.

Logging, as well as the quarrying of limestone and barium lead, in the Merced River Canyon helped keep the railroad running even as passenger business suffered serious declines. But it wasn't enough, and the railroad went out of business.

The highway was constructed in part with convict labor from San Quentin and Folsom Prisons; Briceburg itself was originally the site of a prison camp. Later, the Brice family opened a store and a small resort where the camp had been; today, there is just the bridge, a couple of homes, and an unmanned Bureau of Land Management station. The BLM, along with the Forest Service, manages the Merced as a National Wild and Scenic River.

The paved road on the south side of the canyon continues for about eighteen miles to El Portal; the park entrance is another two miles farther on.

The Savage Trading Post is a few miles shy of El Portal. Visit the Native American crafts shop there, and don't worry about Ned, the Old English sheepdog who stands guard at the entrance: He'll greet you with a bark, but he's a pussycat.

The man who built the trading post, James D. Savage, is infamous for his role in the history of Yosemite. Savage, a charismatic scoundrel who made a fortune as a gold miner and cattle rustler, worked for John Sutter, served under John C. Fremont, and reputedly married more then twenty Native American women.

Savage also organized and led the "Mariposa Battalion," a group of volunteers who pursued the Southern Sierra Miwok (also called the Ahwahneechee), with the intent of removing the tribe from their ancestral home. Savage's men followed the Miwok into a fantastic valley of cliffs, spires, and waterfalls: Yosemite Valley. Dr. Lafayette Bunnell, a doctor attached to the battalion, was struck by the valley's beauty and the plight of its people. At his urging, the land was named Yosemite, the Miwok word for grizzly bear.

Although Savage and his battalion were the first white men to view this valley from

its floor, they were not the first white men to see Yosemite. That honor lay with Joseph Walker, who, in the company of fifty-seven mountain men in 1833, made the first east to west crossing of the Sierra Nevada Mountains by white men. The Walker party viewed the valley and marveled at its wonders, but never left the rim of this "grizzly bear" valley.

Today, Cedar Lodge, four miles past the Savage Trading Post, has a huge bear population on its premises. However, they are all carved wood, including one sporting a camera around his neck. The little gift shop in this pleasant motel features a collection of bears, too, all of them stuffed.

Cedar Lodge is at a place called Incline, once the site of a lumber operation. Look at the top of the ridge across the river from the motel. The Trumbull Peak fire lookout tower is visible against the horizon. Huge slabs of concrete are also visible, just to the right of the fire lookout. These slabs formed the base of the cable railway that brought timber from the high country down to the Merced River and the Yosemite Valley Railway. The remains of another cable railway can be seen a few miles farther, on the south side of the river above El Portal.

Watch the river in spring and summer for rafters and kayakers, who navigate nine miles of white water running west of El Portal, where there are rapids with names like Stark Reality and Ned's Gulch. The river, with deep pools and shallow rapids, runs less wild for seven miles beyond Briceburg.

El Portal

El Portal, Spanish for "the gateway," sits just outside Yosemite National Park, though it is still two thousand feet below and seven miles from Yosemite Valley. The little community serves as the home for many Yosemite park and concessionary employees, and several of the park's administrative offices and a water treatment plant are also located in El Portal, partially screened by trees across the river on Foresta Road.

El Portal, the terminus for the Yosemite Valley Railroad, has a display that includes a locomotive and train cars. El Portal also has a small grocery store and a gas station, as well as a Forest Service campground. It also has the massive Yosemite View Lodge. The sheer bulk of the Lodge makes it seem out of place in this tiny town along a two-lane highway. It would have been better, perhaps, if it could have been tucked out of sight, but it does offer needed lodging space, particularly after some of the accommodations inside Yosemite Valley were damaged by floods in 1997.

Beyond El Portal the road begins a steep ascent into the upper reaches of the Merced River Canyon, passing through a forest of oak, pine, and aspen. The Cascades, an im-

pressive waterfall, is a few miles beyond the western park entrance at the Arch Rock Ranger Station, shooting over the edge of a box canyon on the north side of the road.

About six miles past El Portal the highway intersects with New Big Oak Flat Road. The Merced River here spills over an old dam on the right. Park in the pullout on the left side of the road, just past the junction. Watch the rocks a little above and to the right of the pullout, where climbers can sometimes be seen ascending the granite walls and boulders.

Beyond here Highway 140 levels out and the canyon walls close in. The road continues past ponderosa pines, incense cedars, oaks, and dogwood for a little less than two miles. The All Year Highway, its work finished, ends at the entrance to the Yosemite Valley.

GOLD COUNTRY

Gold in California has been mined from Nevada to the Pacific, from Oregon to Mexico. The precious metal was discovered near Los Angeles long before the start of the gold rush, and enormous amounts of gold were later taken out of the Klamath Mountains in northwest California and in the Great Basin Desert in the eastern part of the state.

But the heart of Gold Country resides along the "Mother Lode Highway," Highway 49, which commemorates the year 1849—the year gold fever reached its peak. Traveling over the oak-covered foothills and pine-clad mountains of the Sierra Nevada for more than three hundred miles, the Mother Lode Highway passes through some of the state's loveliest and most historic places.

The California gold rush, of course, gave Gold Country its name. But the discovery of gold back in 1848 was kept quiet for a little while and did not stir much excitement, even when word leaked to the outside world. Settlers, including former Mexican citizens and newly arrived Americans, were the first to reach the goldfields in the U.S. territory wrested the previous year from Mexico. But the rush was on when the canny Mormon businessman, Sam Brannan, cornered the market on mining equipment and then traveled to San Francisco, where he waved a bottle of gold dust and shouted "Gold from the American River!"

By 1850, two years after the discovery of gold by James Marshall at Sutter's Mill in the remote Coloma Valley of the Sierra Nevada Mountains, one hundred thousand people had flooded into California. Those that experienced the rigors of life during the gold rush were said by Californians to be "seeing the elephant." Miners from Mexico, Chile, and Peru poured in from the south, wagon trains traveled across the Great Plains, ships set sail from New York, and Hawaiians jumped ship in San Francisco. Cornish miners from Great Britain, experts at tunneling deep underground, sailed across the Atlantic in the company of Welsh, Irish, French, and other English argonauts, while Chinese immigrants escaped political and social upheaval by sailing across the Pacific to find their rumored "gold mountain." Yet rampant racism directed toward minorities flourished. And the huge influx of people brought near extermination to California's Native Americans.

Working mining claims from Oakhurst in the south to Sierra City in the north, the immigrants built hundreds of towns and mining camps, hoping to find the "mother lode," the mythical place where all the gold that washed into the streams and rivers had come from originally. The first prospectors panned for gold in the waterways, where the heavy, yellow metal was easy to find. Later, they dug "coyote holes" into ancient, dry streambeds, blasted tunnels into the Sierra bedrock, and developed hydraulic mining techniques that washed away entire mountainsides.

Most of the mining activity in the southern part of this region took place in the foothills, while in the north it was often located at higher elevations. Gold fever cooled by 1859, and today much of the physical evidence of that earlier era has disappeared. But Highway 49 and the connecting scenic backroads make it easy to view much of what does remain. The roads described here sample some of the best-known towns and mining camps along Highway 49, and also explore more remote, less frequently visited corners of Gold Country.

Come, see the elephant . . .

Coulterville

It was late afternoon on an overcast, spring day when I visited Coulterville, once a gold mining camp in the Sierra Nevada foothills. The gold that could be panned from nearby creeks had played out soon enough, but the town, tucked into a small valley, became an important supply center for outlying mining camps scattered across many miles of rugged, steep terrain. Coulterville, which sat over a rich vein of gold, was also the starting point for the first maintained road into Yosemite, and at least a part of that historic road can still be explored.

The town is named for George Coulter, who traveled west from Pennsylvania in a covered wagon with his wife, Margaret. Coulter set up a store along Maxwell Creek, at the future site of Coulterville, saving miners thirty miles of travel for supplies, either to Mariposa, to the south, or Chinese Camp to the north.

On arrival at the creek, Coulter attached a tent to the limb of an oak tree, flew a small American flag from the top of the tent, and opened for business. The town that began to grow up around the store was called Banderita—which means "little flag" in Spanish—by the Mexican miners. Not long after, Banderita became Coulterville.

Coulterville sits along either side of Highway 49, and can be reached from Modesto in the Central Valley, via California Highway 132 (also named Yosemite Boulevard).

A scenic and historic backroad to Coulterville follows California Highway 59 from Merced. The route begins just south of the historic courthouse on N Street, following the course of the defunct Yosemite Valley Railroad on Highway 59.

At the little community of Snelling, about seventeen miles up Highway 59, you can turn right onto County Road J16 heading east, which is also called Merced Falls Road. Continue on the road to reach the community of Merced Falls; the edge of Lake McSwain and the dammed Merced River is just outside of town.

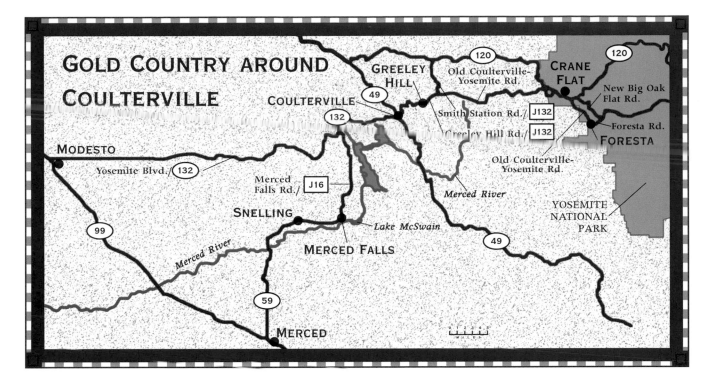

As Merced Falls Road bears north, the ruins of an old lumber mill along the Yosemite Valley Railroad line are visible. The road crosses gently rolling foothills dotted with oaks, and there are good views west of the Central Valley. Merced Falls Road ends at Highway 132, and a right turn leads the last few miles east to Coulterville on Highway 49.

There are forty-seven historic buildings and sites in Coulterville, and every building on Main Street, except one, dates from between the mid-1800s and early 1900s. The most impressive building, constructed in 1851, is the Hotel Jeffery, which first served as a dance hall attended by Mexican miners, and where, according to one disapproving commentator, "a rude native dance" known as the Spanish Fandango was performed by *señoritas* wielding castanets. Later, the dance hall served as a stagecoach stop and hotel for tourists traveling to Yosemite. President Theodore Roosevelt was among the more prominent visitors to the hotel; his 1902 signature can be seen in the hotel register, which is on display in the lobby. Roosevelt was on his way to meet John Muir, who founded the Sierra Club.

George Jeffery (his name is misspelled as

"Jeffrey" in the town cemetery) built the hotel. The Jeffery family repaired the building each time it was damaged by fire until, in its final incarnation, the Jeffery became the grand, three-story hotel that stands today. The Magnolia Saloon, a restored gold rush-era watering hole, is next door to the hotel.

The Wells Fargo Store, across Highway 49 from the Jeffery, dates to 1856. A little steam locomotive, the "Whistling Billy," is near the store. The locomotive once traveled along a four-mile stretch of track known as "The Crookedest Railroad in the World,"

COULTERVILLE, LOOKING EASTWARD, WITH THE HOTEL JEFFERY DATING FROM 1851, ON THE LEFT.

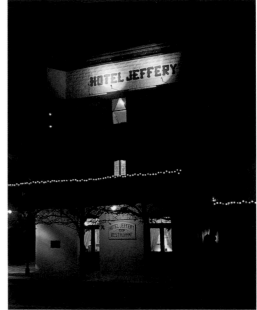

ABOVE, LEFT:
SUNSET TURNS THE SUN
SUN WO COMPANY
STORE TO GOLD IN
COULTERVILLE.

ABOVE, RIGHT:
THE HOTEL JEFFERY IN
COULTERVILLE LIT UP
FOR THE EVENING.

shuttling between the nearby Mary Harrison Mine and the gold processing mill. The locomotive sits beneath the "Hanging Tree," where Leon Ruiz was hanged in 1856 for the robbery and murder of two Chinese miners. The Northern Mariposa History Center, with old photographs and mining exhibits, is in the remains of the Coulterville Hotel.

By 1853, the town had twenty-five saloons, ten hotels, and perhaps five thousand inhabitants representing nine nationalities. About fifteen hundred inhabitants of Coulterville were Chinese and one of them, Mon Da Sun, built the Sun Sun Wo Company in 1851, a store that still stands.

Like so many other California towns in the 1800s, Coulterville suffered the ravages of fire. It burned three times, each fire occurring in July, twenty years apart, in 1859, 1879, and 1899, and each time the town was rebuilt. The one building to survive the conflagrations was the Sun Sun Wo Company store. It's adobe construction made it impervious to fire.

According to local legend, a long-departed citizen hid a crude, leather pouch—a poke—of gold coins in the walls of his home, and the remains from the building, which burned in the town's last fire, were later used to fill potholes in the dirt streets. Gold coins appeared with the first winter rains, precipitating Coulterville's wild "Gold Rush of 1899," when Coulterville's residents literally tore up the streets.

Greeley Hill Road and the Old Coulterville-Yosemite Road

The Old Coulterville-Yosemite Road was the first road into Yosemite. Until the route was completed, Yosemite was only accessible to the hardiest of travelers. In August, 1913, the road took on new significance when automobiles, banned from the park since 1907, were allowed into Yosemite Valley over the Coulterville Road, as it was then called. Teams and saddle horses had the right of way, and the speed limit on straight stretches was ten miles per hour. That summer, 127 cars made the arduous journey.

Part of the road to Yosemite past Coulterville can still be followed today. To travel the section of the road that can be easily navigated by a passenger car, obtain a Stanislaus National Forest map, published by the U.S. Forest Service. Most other maps do not correctly show the Old Coulterville-Yosemite Road.

Our tour here begins on Greeley Hill Road (County Road J132), east of Coulterville. The road travels eight miles over gentle foothills, and then up several steep grades covered in chaparral. Watch for fenceposts with innumerable holes that were drilled by acorn woodpeckers. Many of the holes do, in fact, hold acorns.

Greeley Hill, once the site of a Native

CALIFORNIA SKETCH: THE SUN KOW FAMILY

The history of the Sun and Moy Kow family began fifty years before this photograph was taken at the beginning of the twentieth century. In 1849, Mon Da Sun, Sun Kow's father, heard the stories trickling into China that America was a land of limitless opportunities. China, by contrast, was a land of diminished opportunities, having been weakened by the opportunistic intervention of England and France in its affairs. In southern China, where the elder Sun lived, the poor were starving, and a revolution was imminent. A few people decided to take a chance on new, if uncertain, lives and emigrated to America. When word came that gold had been discovered in California, the "few" leaving China became many.

As violence spread across southern China, Mon Da Sun left his family and his country to look for what the Chinese called the "gold mountain." Like most Chinese who made the trip, he probably arrived in San Francisco first, and then traveled on to Sacramento. Those Chinese who worked as miners would go to Auburn, a town in the Sierra Nevada foothills, then to the goldfields along the American River. Later, they would spread two hundred miles north and south along the Mother Lode.

Sun made enough money from the goldfields to finance five trips to China. But he wasn't a miner for long: He opened a general store in Coulterville in 1851. A few years later, he invited his twenty-year-old son, Sun Kow, to California to help manage the growing business, headquartered in the adobe building that became known as the Sun Sun Wo Company store. Mon Da Sun returned to China before his death.

Sun Kow stayed in California and wed in an arranged marriage with Moy Leong, a young woman from China. The Kows had five daughters, all of whom remained in the United States. The photograph made around 1900 of Sun and Moy, posed with their first daughter, Minnie, shows a mixture of cultural symbols from east and west. Sitting between her parents and held firmly in the grasp of her father, Minnie appears to be the most poised member of the trio, simultaneously confident, relaxed and indifferent to the blend of two cultures that surrounds her.

The Kows later moved to the town of Isleton, in the Sacramento Delta. Sun, ill with diabetes, reversed the path his father had made long ago. He left his own family and returned to China, where he died about year later. Moy died on the same day, a half a world away.

ABOVE:

SUN AND MOY KOW AND THEIR FIRST DAUGHTER, MINNIE, CIRCA 1900. (COURTESY OF DANNY MOYERS.)

American camp, is nestled in a valley surrounded by meadows and pine forests. A sign at the west end of the community reads, "Greeley Hill: Population Friendly, Elevation Just Right." The town was settled by two brothers who were relatives of Horace Greeley. Perhaps they had followed the famous writer's advice to "Go west, young man." Family legend has it that Horace Greeley visited his relatives in Greeley Hill when he traveled to Yosemite.

Several side roads branch out from Greeley Hill and lead past old homes and barns, but care should be taken on the dirt roads, which can be treacherously muddy. Some roads are submerged by overflowing

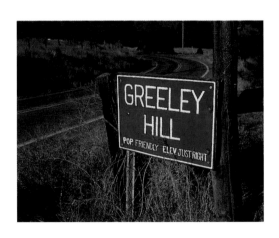

GREELEY HILL:
POPULATION FRIENDLY,
ELEVATION JUST RIGHT.

creeks during winter and spring.

The Greeley Lumber Mill which sat on a hill and gave the community its name, is no longer operational, but look for the still-functioning Schutt Lumber Mill on Ernst Road, just outside of town. Owned and operated by the Schutt family for more than fifty years, the property today is littered with remnants of a bygone age. A Model A Ford has been turned into a mini-sawmill, there are logging trucks built in 1942, and an old International Harvester tractor rests quietly, its red paint faded from too many years sitting out in the sun and rain.

There are only a few services in Greeley Hill, most located just off the highway, including some restaurants, a market and gas station, and a hardware store.

A few miles east of Greeley Hill, Greeley Hill Road reaches an intersection with Smith Station Road, which leads up through the forest to Highway 120. Stay on Greeley Hill Road for another mile or so and you will end up where the Old Coulterville-Yosemite Road (Forest Service Road 2S01) begins. This is a good place to call a halt if you don't have a good map (such as the Stanislaus National Forest map). The road from here is poorly

marked and there are innumerable logging roads that branch off the Old Coulterville-Yosemite Road, some of them more suitable for four-wheel-drive vehicles. The road is dirt from here on out, all the way into Yosemite National Park.

Followed to its conclusion, the Old Coulterville-Yosemite Road eventually reaches Yosemite National Park at the little community of Foresta, where there is a private inholding of perhaps a dozen homes, but no services. But road washouts and periodically locked gates make completing a journey along the Old Coulterville-Yosemite Road problematic.

To reach Foresta on paved roads from Coulterville, take Smith Station Road up to Highway 120 and the New Big Oak Flat Road. At Crane Flat, there is a gas station and general store that are open year round.

Take New Big Oak Flat Road and continue toward Yosemite Valley. Watch on your right for Foresta Road a few miles past Crane Flat. Follow the road down to the aptly named Big Meadow, where there are two restored big red barns on the site of the historic McCauley Ranch. There is also evidence of an enormous fire that swept through the western reaches of the park in 1988.

At the barns, Foresta Road bears to the left and ends about a quarter of a mile later. At one time Foresta Road dropped down into the Merced River Canyon to reach Highway 140, but the road was abandoned after rock falls repeatedly closed it. Bear left at the barns to reach the start of the Old Coulterville-Yosemite Road, which beckons those with sport utility vehicles (SUVs) or mountain bikes.

Nevada City

With its assortment of elegant homes, churches, commercial buildings, and even historic firehouses, Nevada City reigns unchallenged as the gold rush exemplar of architectural restoration and preservation. The means for creating this authentic repository of primarily Victorian-era architecture, much of it dating from the 1850s and 1860s, came from the goldfields discovered at Deer Creek, the future site of Nevada City.

From California Highway 49/20, exit onto Broad Street, the logical place to begin a tour of the town. Drive, or better yet, take a horse-drawn carriage or walk Broad Street and the other streets. The 1855 National Hotel, at the base of Broad Street, is an impressive, three-story brick building with a long, white balcony, a pleasant dining room with a Victorian decor, and a friendly tavern. The New York Hotel, which dates from 1857, no longer entertains guests, but it does house several specialty shops. It's up the hill on Broad Street, next to the red-brick Firehouse Number 2, which was built in 1861. The Nevada Theatre, built in 1865, is across the street from the firehouse.

Firehouse Number 1, also built in 1861, is on Main Street, near the bottom of town. The white frame and brick building has an intricate gingerbread facade (also known as "carpenter's lace"). Now the building houses the Nevada County Historical Society Museum, with a number of artifacts and exhibits from the ill-fated Donner Party, Chinese immigrants, and the gold rush.

There are many places to spend the night in Nevada City, including the aforementioned National Hotel. The inexpensive, tree-shaded Miners Inn is located on Zion Street, about a fifteen-minute walk from the center of town. This single-story motel, dating to the 1940s, includes five cottages named for historic Sierra Nevada gold mines. Three of the cottages were originally miners' cabins, and all of them feature Victorian architecture and decor.

Other interesting styles of architecture, including Colonial and Greek Revival can be found in Nevada City. An example of California Gothic can be seen in the four-story Red Castle, a sumptuous bed-and-breakfast inn built in 1857 on Prospect Hill. It is reputedly the oldest surviving brick home in Nevada City. The current owner, Mary

RANCH NEAR OLD COULTERVILLE-YOSEMITE ROAD, EAST OF GREELEY HILL.

Weaver, graciously gave me a tour. She told me the elegant mansion, when it was built, was visible from much of town. Over the years, pine trees have grown tall enough to obscure the view, and now the Red Castle can only be seen by those willing to find their way up Prospect Hill.

Not all the buildings in Nevada City conform to the gold rush motif. The facades of city hall and the courthouse, for example, are art deco. By the late 1960s, Nevada City passed laws to maintain the town's historic architectural styles. In addition, power lines in the center of the city were buried, and downtown streets were lined with gas lamps.

There was nothing to restore or preserve in 1848 at Deer Creek when James Marshall, who had touched off the gold rush at Sutter's Mill earlier in the year, tried prospecting here. He had no luck finding more of the precious metal, but he left Deer Creek too soon, for other miners later found rich placer deposits of gold in the waterway. Deer Creek Diggings, a mining camp dotted with tents and log cabins, shot up. The camp name changed to Caldwell's Upper Store to honor a popular merchant who opened a branch store at the mining camp. Rich, auriferous gravel deposits were also discovered in the streambed, and dozens of "coyote holes" were dug to reach the gold, just as a coyote will dig furiously to extract a mouse or gopher from a burrow. A second town, Coyoteville, grew just to the northeast of Nevada City, adjacent to these mining holes. Coyote Street remains in Nevada City, but Coyoteville has disappeared.

By the end of 1850, Deer Creek Diggings, now a town with six thousand residents,

was renamed Nevada, the Spanish word for "snow covered." After California joined the Union in 1850, the town of Nevada became the county seat of the newly created Nevada County. The town's name was officially changed to Nevada City in 1864 to avoid confusion with the new state of Nevada.

Miners at Nevada City would end their day walking up the hills around Deer Creek to their cabins, following trails that branched out in all directions. Some of the trails eventually became the paved roads that today traverse the seven hills of Nevada City, and the pattern of streets has been likened to the spokes on a wheel radiating out from a central hub.

The placer gold deposits were exhausted in Nevada City by 1860, although hard-rock mining (mining underground) continued until 1942. Hydraulic mining was invented near Nevada City in 1852, when a French-Canadian miner, Antoine Chabot, used a

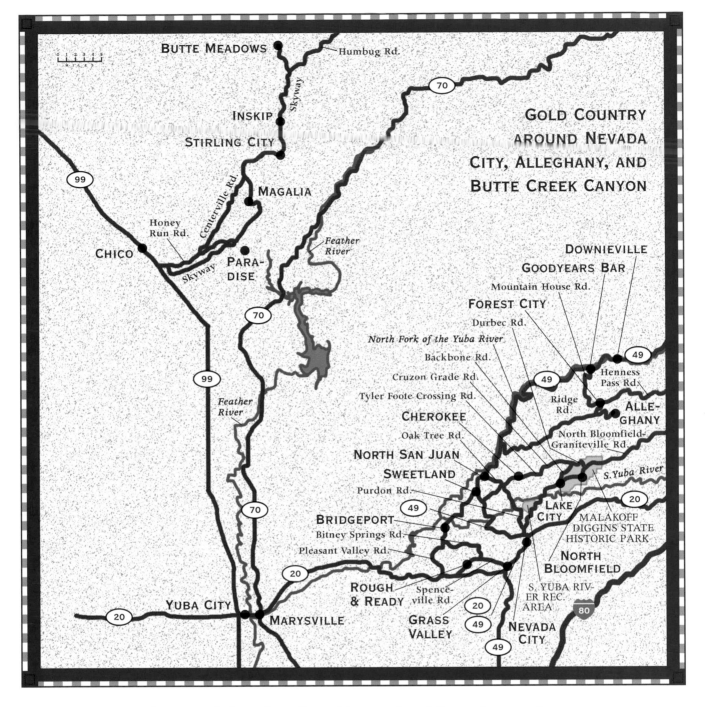

GOLD COUNTRY AROUND NEVADA CITY, ALLEGHANY, AND BUTTE CREEK CANYON

forty-foot-long canvas hose to wash dirt and gravel into a sluice box. Doing so eliminated the need to build a flume or dig a ditch to bring water to dry diggings.

The next year, Edward Mattison, a Connecticut miner, attached a tin nozzle to the end of a rawhide hose. Narrowing the opening of the hose created a much stronger force of water to use against the earth on Mattison's claim. Soon other miners were emulating Mattison's method. In time, rivers and streams were dammed, their waters diverted into canals and flumes that surged through giant water cannons, called monitors. The monitors collapsed entire hillsides in the search for gold that existed not as nuggets or in hard-rock veins, but as fine particles buried in layers of sediment that overlay the Sierra bedrock. The muddy flow of water tumbled through a sluice that could catch heavier particles of gravel containing gold.

As surface deposits of gold were depleted, hydraulic mining became the only

ABOVE:
BROAD STREET IN
NEVADA CITY GLOWS
WITH THE COLOR OF
GOLD AT SUNRISE.

RIGHT:
A HORSE POSES ALONG
BITNEY SPRINGS ROAD,
ABOUT HALFWAY
BETWEEN GRASS VALLEY
AND THE BRIDGEPORT
COVERED BRIDGE.

way to excavate the precious mineral. But the expense of hydraulic mining required enormous financial resources that, ironically, put individuals like Chabot and Mattison out of business. Although Chabot and Mattison probably couldn't imagine it at the time, hydraulic mining would have a profound effect on California's landscape.

The logical conclusion of what hydraulic mining could accomplish is visible about sixteen miles from Nevada City, at Malakoff Diggins State Historic Park. From 1866 until 1884, this was the site of the largest hydraulic mine operation in the world, and it created an unparalleled ecological disaster in California.

Before departing for Malakoff Diggins, a side trip to Grass Valley and the Bridgeport Covered Bridge is in order. Take Zion Street south, which turns into the Nevada City Highway just before it enters Grass Valley. Once in Grass Valley, the highway becomes East Main Street, which will take you through the center of town.

Grass Valley doesn't have the Victorian charm of Nevada City, with its mix of old and new architecture. It does, however, have many historic landmarks, including the nearby Empire Mine State Historic Park, one of the richest gold mines in California. The park includes offices and shops, the hard-rock mine shaft, and the Empire Cottage, a mansion that was the summer residence of the mine owner.

From the western edge of town, follow West Main Street a few miles to reach Bitney Springs Road. The old, rural road leads through the foothills, passing the fresh water bubbling out of Bitney Springs, where locals often stop to fill water jugs. Make a right onto Pleasant Valley Road and stop at the Bridgeport Covered Bridge, which was built in 1862. The 251-foot span over the South Yuba River is the longest covered bridge in the United States.

Continuing past the bridge on Pleasant Valley Road eventually leads to the town of Sweetland on Highway 49, about eighteen miles north of Nevada City. Or retrace your route and return to Grass Valley via Pleasant Valley Road, which intersects with Highway 20. Heading north on Spenceville Road from Highway 20 allows you to stop for a soda at the general store in the community of Rough and Ready. Named after General Zachary "Old Rough and Ready" Taylor, a hero of the Mexican War, the once bustling town briefly seceded from the United States in 1850 to protest a mining tax.

Once back in Grass Valley, consider trying a pasty (pronounced PASS-tee), the local dish introduced during the gold rush by miners from Cornwall, England. The wives would pack their husbands' lunches in tin pails filled with hot tea and these meat pies, which were covered in a baked crust folded over on itself.

The North Bloomfield–Graniteville Road

The North Bloomfield–Graniteville Road is only partially paved with good intentions, because much of the route is over dirt, some of it washboard. But despite the roughness of the route, this historic backroad to Malakoff Diggins will reward you with breathtaking scenery.

To reach North Bloomfield–Graniteville Road from Nevada City, take Broad Street northwest to a Y intersection at East Broad Street, and turn right. East Broad becomes North Bloomfield–Graniteville Road where it crosses Highway 49.

As soon as it leaves Nevada City, North Bloomfield–Graniteville Road passes through a thick forest of pines and oaks that surrounds a quiet, residential neighborhood. A mile or so past Highway 49, the two-lane road suddenly becomes one lane and crosses into the South Yuba River Recreation Area, which contains trails and campgrounds under the jurisdiction of the federal Bureau of Land Management. The road begins a steep, switchbacked descent through the pines and dogwood toward the river, reaching the canyon bottom and the beautiful Edwards Crossing Bridge about eight miles from Highway 49. Built in 1904, the Edwards

SWIMMERS TAKE TO THE WATERS OF THE SOUTH YUBA RIVER BELOW THE EDWARDS CROSSING BRIDGE, ON THE NORTH BLOOMFIELD–GRANITEVILLE ROAD.

dredges have to be carried to the water, sometimes for miles.

The route beyond the bridge is unpaved, although my wife and I had no trouble negotiating it with our passenger vehicle. The route led up the side of the canyon for about one and one-half steep miles, reaching a junction with Grizzly Hill Road, which travels down the mountain toward Highway 49. But we continued on North Bloomfield–Graniteville Road and reached the South Yuba River Campground.

We were a little concerned we wouldn't be able to find an open campsite, even during midweek, but we needn't have worried. Only one of the fifteen campsites scattered around two loops was occupied, and we were the last people to arrive that day. We discovered that the campground also serves as a trailhead to the Malakoff Diggins in one direction, and the river, in the other. We chose one of several large sites screened off from the rest of the campground by pine trees and manzanita bushes.

I walked beyond our camp to collect some of the abundant downed wood for our campfire, while our little dog, Beau, chased a squirrel. I saw a steep, thirty-foot-high hillside denuded of vegetation, apparently by hydraulic mining. I knew it was only a small sample of what to expect the next morning.

That night we pulled out our little camp stove and had soup, crackers, cheese, and fruit for dinner, and wondered what the first placer miners would have dined on. After dinner we met our fellow campers, two gentlemen from Arizona who had spent the day dredging for gold above the Edwards Crossing Bridge. Then Kathy and I sat next to our campfire under a moonless, starry sky. We were serenaded by croaking frogs and the crackle of our fire, and when a pack of howling coyotes chimed in, Beau, who had fallen asleep, perked up his ears.

In the morning, after downing some strong coffee—one item we could be sure the miners would have enjoyed, too—we drove about two miles from our campground to reach a junction with Lake City Road,

Crossing Bridge is the second replacement for the original bridge that dated to 1850 and brought miners from Nevada City to the Malakoff Diggins over the South Yuba River Toll Road. Today, the 114-foot bridge, with an unusual three-hinged metal arch, can be traversed for free.

There are a few pullouts along either side of the bridge and several unofficial paths lead down to the river, which is popular with waders and swimmers—at least when water levels aren't too high. Recreational gold dredging is allowed for a few miles above and below the bridge. The South Yuba can only be reached by foot trails here, and

which offered another roundabout route back to Highway 49. The terrain was flatter, here, with open fields all around. Communities sprang up anywhere two roads met, and such was the case at Lake City. Nothing remains today except a sign marking the spot where less than one hundred people lived in 1857. Near the sign is an odd, fifteen-foot-high, whimsical metal sculpture of three daffodils, the unofficial flower of Gold Country.

Malakoff

The road crossed onto the three thousand acres of the Malakoff Diggins State Historic Park just past Lake City. The name of the park apparently originates from an 1857 mining claim made by A. Malakoff and Company. "Diggins" was the slang term used by the miners and is now employed by the park.

We stopped at the park's first official viewpoint, the Western Diggins Overlook, where we began to understand the extent of the hydraulic mining operations at Malakoff. The view was to the northeast, and we looked down into an excavated pit that is over 7,000-feet long, 3,000-feet wide, and 300-feet deep. The pit was weirdly beautiful, though the colorful, delicate-looking landforms at Malakoff were created by miners with monitors, not Mother Nature. The landscape was shaped by the force of water, which was transported via ditches and flumes from the mountains above. By the time the water had dropped with the force of gravity to the diggings, it had the power to blast the hills to smithereens.

To the northeast, where the pit bent out of sight, enormous, pleated hillsides reminded us of Bryce Canyon in Utah or the badlands of Death Valley. We hiked down a short trail to reach the inner edge of the diggings; our trail connected with others that lead throughout the park. We stopped to look at an old monitor, which was still aimed at its defenseless target. The monitors, using powerful jets of water operated by one or two men, blasted away hundreds of tons of earth and gravel every day, twenty-four

hours a day. We saw more of what hydraulic mining had done as we wandered farther into the pit, where we could see the bare, wrinkled hillside, looking like columns of earth stretching up to the pine trees on the rim of the pit.

Once back in our car we drove east from the overlook, passing the Humbug Trail that follows Humbug Creek back to the South Yuba River Campground. Next we passed over the 556-foot Hiller Tunnel, built to carry the sludge out of the diggings and send it down toward the Central Valley. The tunnel can be entered by those with a sense of adventure, a flashlight, and rubber-soled shoes.

The Diggins Overlook is just beyond the tunnel, but over the years pine trees have grown to obscure much of the view. The privately owned Crystal Hill Mine is on the opposite side of the road.

North Bloomfield

We continued on North Bloomfield–Graniteville Road through little North Bloomfield, once a thriving town that served the mining community and now largely a museum. The roadway was lined in places with poppies and the pink-petaled farewell-to-spring.

The town was first named Humbug in 1851 by miners who looked for gold there, without luck. Later, when gold finally was discovered, the town was renamed North Bloomfield. There is not a South Bloomfield nor Bloomfield nearby; "North" was added to the town's name to distinguish it from the Sonoma County town of Bloomfield. The town might have remained Humbug, except that same year, 1857, seven towns applied to the U.S. Postal Service with that name.

Today, North Bloomfield has about a block of restored buildings that look as they did during the gold rush when some eight hundred people lived here, including miners and those who served the miners. Kathy and I visited the McKillican and Mobley Store (pronounce it so that "Mob" rhymes with "Bob" and you'll sound like a local), which is stocked with merchandise typical

ABOVE:
AN UNNATURAL, IF
WEIRDLY BEAUTIFUL,
LANDSCAPE—THE
REMNANTS OF HYDRAU-
LIC MINING AT
MALAKOFF DIGGINS
STATE PARK.

RIGHT:
HYDRAULIC MINING
BLASTS AWAY AT
MALAKOFF DIGGINS,
CIRCA 1875. (PHOTO-
GRAPH COURTESY THE
NORTH STAR MINING
MUSEUM.)

of the nineteenth century when the shop served as a general store and post office.

Just past North Bloomfield, and still on the North Bloomfield–Graniteville Road, we drove into Chute Hill Campground, named for a flume that brought water from the high country to Malakoff. The comfortable campground, surrounded by pines, has thirty family sites and a group site. Stopping near site 27, Kathy and I walked a few yards downhill to a flat spot and a bench. The trees were cleared away, with most of Malakoff Diggins spread out before us in one, panoramic view. From this overlook, Kathy and I could see just how incredibly gold mining affected the land here.

The damage inflicted on the landscape by the North Bloomfield Gravel Mining Company is nothing compared to what happened downstream. An enormous amount of water flowed to the Diggins from a network of reservoirs, flumes, and drainage tunnels that ran under the mountains. The water, once it had done its work at the Diggins, reached the Central Valley and deposited its load of gravel loosed by the hydraulic mining—called tailings—in riverbeds. The bed of the Yuba River, where it ran through Marysville, rose seventy feet over thirty-one years, to a level higher than the city itself. The water could not always be contained, despite the construction of a levee system. Both the town and surrounding farmland were flooded with water and tons of rock debris. Navigation was also imperiled along the Sacramento River and even in the San Francisco Bay.

The ecological disaster resulted in a landmark lawsuit against the North Bloomfield Gravel Mining Company. Judge Lorenzo Sawyer sided with mining opponents and ended large-scale hydraulic mining in California in 1884 by issuing a permanent injunction against the dumping of tailings into California's waterways. This was the first judgment in favor of environmental protection in the United States.

Antoine Chabot, the man who turned the

first hose on the dry diggings, was not proud of the part he played in the invention of hydraulic mining and spent much of the remainder of his life making amends. He became more interested in water than gold. Chabot understood that the power of water had less to do with how much of it came out of a hose nozzle than who had the right to use it. He moved to the east side of San Francisco Bay, where he changed his name to Anthony Chabot. A philanthropist, he amassed a fortune by developing and controlling several East Bay water systems. Lake Chabot, which he built, Chabot Observatory, which he endowed, as well as Chabot Regional Park and Chabot College are, among other East Bay locations, named in his honor.

ABOVE, TOP:
THE MCKILLICAN AND MOBLEY STORE IN NORTH BLOOMFIELD.

ABOVE, BOTTOM:
MINERS POSE FOR A GROUP PORTRAIT AT THE DURBEC MINE AT NORTH BLOOMFIELD. NOTE THE "TEA COZY," A LUNCH PAIL HELD BY THE CHILD IN THE FRONT ROW, FIRST USED BY WELSH MINERS (WHO SPECIALIZED IN HARD-ROCK MINING); A COZY KEPT A MINER'S TEA AND PASTIES WARM.

Routes Back to Nevada City

Highway 49 and Nevada City can be reached by paved roads that avoid retracing your path along the North Bloomfield–Graniteville Road. The route begins at North Bloomfield and continues around Chute Hill Campground on the North Bloomfield–Graniteville Road, heading north. Turn left onto Durbec Road, and left again onto Backbone Road. The pavement begins about a mile up Backbone Road past Chute Campground, at Cruzon Grade Road, which plummets steeply down the mountain to Tyler Foote Crossing Road. A left turn onto Tyler Foote leads past the site of North Columbia, where you can see the Coughlin House, built in 1875, and used as a stagecoach stop. The house was rebuilt in 1921 after the original structure was destroyed by fire. We met the current owner, Mary Campbell, who served as the teacher in the one-room schoolhouse that still stands across the road from the Coughlin House. Today, the house is used as a cultural center for the surrounding community.

Beyond North Columbia we reached the blighted landscape at Cherokee, where more hydraulic mining was carried out, though on a much smaller scale than at Malakoff. The bare, chalky-white soil and ponds of dark green water give Cherokee an otherworldly look.

A few miles past Cherokee, Tyler Foote Crossing Road reaches yet another intersection. Oak Tree Road on the right leads northwest to Highway 49 and the community of North San Juan, where there is a gas station, two groceries, a tavern, and a restaurant. Purdon Road, a rough dirt road on the left, runs down a hill and crosses the South Fork of the Yuba River, eventually finding its way to Nevada City. The Tyler Foote Crossing Road also reaches Highway 49 south of North San Juan, with Nevada City eleven miles to the south.

A SIGN IN THE WINDOW OF THE GOLD RUSH–ERA BEUREN AND CHISM GENERAL STORE IN NORTH SAN JUAN, NOW AN AUTO REPAIR GARAGE OPERATED BY BARNEY LUSK.

Before we left the Malakoff Diggins State Historic Park that summer day, Kathy and I stopped in at the park headquarters and museum, which long ago was the North Bloomfield Dance Hall. The ranger told us people still pan the nearby Humbug Creek.

"Sometimes," the ranger told us, "people still find gold."

Humbug Creek lived up to its name, as we failed to find any precious, yellow metal in our pans. But we considered ourselves lucky, nonetheless, for having explored the North Bloomfield–Graniteville Road.

The Ridge Road to Alleghany

There is an honest charm to Alleghany, the last hard-rock gold mining town in operation in California. The town sits high above Highway 49, in the Sierra Nevada Mountains southwest of Downieville. Like the gold hidden beneath the town, Alleghany's charm must sometimes be mined.

I began my trip to Alleghany one summer day, driving north four miles from North San Juan, along Highway 49. A right turn put me onto the Ridge Road, which imme-

Alleghany

Meanwhile, the Ridge Road contours down and around Pliocene Ridge. The forest thins on the downslope side of the road; other pine-covered ridges are visible to the south and southeast. Then Ridge Road enters Alleghany Canyon, and after three miles, Alleghany itself comes into view, half hidden by trees and clinging to the steep, forested sides of the mountain. There are a few dozen homes and one commercial street with a little museum, a post office, a bar called Casey's Place, and the Red Star Café.

Unfortunately, many of the town's gold rush buildings on Main Street, including the hotel and saloon, were destroyed in a 1983 fire. There are no gas stations, no places to buy fast food, no banks or Laundromats, no hotels. Alleghany is primarily about gold mining, not tourism.

Gold was discovered in 1852 in streams near Alleghany. The find was made by Hawaiian sailors, who, suffering from gold fever, jumped ship. The town received its name from a subsequent group of Pennsylvania miners. They intentionally spelled the name of the town as "Alleghany," rather than the Pennsylvanian "Allegheny," to both identify with and differentiate themselves from their home state. The placer gold in the streams was soon depleted. Yet there was still plenty of gold; it was just well concealed in white veins of quartz beneath Alleghany. Underground mining, more properly known as hard-rock mining, was underway next, with miners tunneling and blasting deep into the earth. The most famous mine was and still is the Original Sixteen to One, named after a campaign slogan given in speeches by presidential candidate William Jennings Bryan in 1896, in which he advocated mixing sixteen parts of silver to one part of gold in U.S. coinage.

LOOKING UP THE RIDGE ROAD ON THE WAY TO ALLEGHANY.

diately began to switchback up through pines and oaks until it reached a junction with the Pike City Road. I discovered there is no longer a city at Pike, only a collection of homes and ranches and a welter of rough dirt roads that I decided to leave for a subsequent visit.

Past the Pike City Road intersection, the Ridge Road straightens out as it travels east over the spine of the massive Pliocene Ridge. The few signs of civilization include the Pliocene School, where the student body, from kindergarten through high school, numbers fewer than one hundred.

After about sixteen miles, the Ridge Road reaches an intersection with Mountain House Road. This road, mostly dirt, grazes Forest City, a tiny mining town that still has its historic dance hall. The road then makes a spectacular drop down the mountain to Highway 49 and the community of Goodyears Bar. A few miles east is the town of Downieville, along the North Fork of the Yuba River, where modern-day gold miners operate dredges in the search for gold. Henness Pass Road, a mostly dirt route that eventually reaches distant Highway 89 to the east, also connects with the Ridge Road at the Mountain House Junction.

ABOVE, TOP:
DREDGING FOR GOLD
ALONG THE NORTH FORK
OF THE YUBA RIVER
NEAR DOWNIEVILLE,
NEXT TO HIGHWAY 49.

ABOVE, BOTTOM:
LOOKING OUT THE
ORIGINAL SIXTEEN TO
ONE MINE SHAFT
ENTRANCE IN
ALLEGHANY.

Just past the museum I turned right, onto Little Kanaka Creek Road. A patch of ground contained a few cars that were almost completely covered in vines. Beyond the automobile graveyard the road dropped into a narrow canyon with several collapsed mine buildings. The hillside along the road was pocked here and there with mine shafts. I reached the bottom of the canyon and the creek, but past here the rough road requires four-wheel drive, and so I turned around.

I stopped for coffee at the Red Star, named for a vein of quartz that runs beneath the cafe. The rock wall at the back of the building is the only artifact on Main Street that survived the 1983 fire.

I was the only tourist in town. The Red Star's manager told me the only other people likely to sit out on the café porch that day would be some of the miners, including her husband, after they finished their shift at 4 P.M. Before leaving the mine, the manager told me the miners had to strip naked before changing from work to street clothes, to prevent "high grading," the mining term for the theft of gold.

Various tours of the mine can be arranged in advance through the museum. At the company's in-town office I saw some of the jewelry produced and sold by the mine; gold is also smelted and poured into bars. Then I traveled down the side of the mountain in a "crummy," an old car used to take miners to the entrance of the mine shaft. The entrance itself looks like a set out of a movie. The main shaft drops down twenty-seven hundred feet and then branches out in all directions for many more thousands of feet. On my tour, I only went a short distance past the opening, although other tours descend almost to the bottom of the mine.

Somehow, as I realized when I got back to town, I left a camera lens near the mine entrance. I knew I would disrupt the normal activities of people at the mine if I were to ask them to look for my lens in the afternoon. I assumed someone would find it anyway. I still had plenty of camera gear, so I continued wandering around town making

It's always boom or bust for the Original Sixteen to One, because hard-rock mining relies primarily on the discovery of high-grade ore inside the veins of quartz. "The gold won't run out in our lifetime," the mine's accessible and on-site president and CEO, Michael Miller, told me. "The difficulty," he added, "is in locating and extracting it."

I wandered by the Alleghany Mining Museum. Across the street was a house with a long front porch, which served at one time as the town morgue. Miners who died in the winter were stored, without need for refrigeration, in the building until spring, when they could be buried in town or transported down the mountain.

pictures, thinking I'd call the mine office the next day.

Bud Buezkowske, a transplant from the San Francisco Bay Area, saw me wandering around town and introduced himself. He pointed me toward the old Catholic church, which was hidden behind a few dilapidated houses, and to the town cemetery, also hidden from easy view.

By the time I finished exploring Alleghany it was almost 4 P.M. I climbed into my car and started to drive away from the Red Star Café when I spotted a car coming from the direction of the mine. Somehow, I knew my missing lens was in that car. As if read-ing each other's minds, the other driver and I both slowed to a halt opposite each other. I extended my arm. Without a word, the driver in the other car extended his arm, too, and put my camera lens in my open hand.

No one has to worry too much that the men and women who plumb the depths of the Original Sixteen to One mine will "high grade" the gold. The only concern anyone in Alleghany should have is that too many tourists might overwhelm the honest charms of the last hard-rock gold mine town in Cali-fornia.

A SPECTACULAR FLOWER GARDEN IN THE TOWN OF ALLEGHANY.

THE HONEY RUN ROAD
COVERED BRIDGE IN
BUTTE CREEK CANYON;
ANCIENT CASCADE LAVA
FLOWS ARE VISIBLE IN
THE UPPER RIGHT OF
THE PICTURE.

Butte Creek Canyon and the Centerville Road

When I was a college student I would occasionally drive a few miles with my girlfriend to the Honey Run Road Covered Bridge in Butte Creek Canyon, not far from Chico State. We would walk across the bridge, listening to our footsteps echo inside the wooden span, listening to the water flowing beneath us, and then share a kiss in the night gone suddenly very still.

It's been a long time since I've kissed anyone at the covered bridge. But I have been back—in daylight—to enjoy the history and picturesque scenery of Butte Creek Canyon that I didn't quite care as much about when I was in college.

To reach the mouth of Butte Creek Canyon from California Highway 99, take the Skyway exit in Chico, drive northeast about a mile and a half, and turn left onto Honey Run Road. (The Skyway continues to the town of Paradise, traveling up the ridge that is the south wall of Butte Creek Canyon.) Honey Run Road quickly enters Butte Creek Canyon and travels beneath a canopy of oaks, liquid amber (sweetgum), and digger pines, following along the north side of Butte

Creek. The black cliffs above the road are ancient lava flows that originated far to the north in the Cascade Range. Those flows, which continued for millions of years, cover the even older Sierra bedrock, which is exposed at the bottom of the canyon. Butte Creek Canyon is, then, a meeting place between two great mountain ranges.

Honey Run Road continues for about four and a half miles, passing by occasional ranches, homes, and rock walls until it reaches the covered bridge and a junction with the Centerville Road. The Honey Run Road Covered Bridge, which was originally used by horse-drawn wagons and then automobiles and now carries only foot traffic, is at the confluence of Big Butte and Little Butte Creeks; it's one of twelve remaining covered bridges in California. Until it was built in 1886, the creeks had to be crossed by fording the often raging water.

The covered bridge served well for many years, but today a new steel and concrete bridge, just upstream, handles vehicle traffic. The old covered bridge is a popular place for picnics during the warmer months of the year. It's often deserted midweek and during the winter.

Honey Run Road crosses the new bridge and climbs the side of the canyon over five miles of twisting, single-lane road, to rejoin the Skyway at Paradise. Along the way there are grand views of both Butte Creek Canyon and Little Butte Creek Canyon. The town of Paradise is spread along a pine-covered ridge. From the town, the Skyway can be followed up into the Sierra Nevada Mountains to the little communities of Magalia, Stirling City, and Inskip. Just beyond Inskip, there's a fork in the road. The Skyway, on the left, travels to Butte Meadows, which is a little forest community a few miles off of California Highway 32. The right fork is Humbug Road, where the pavement becomes dirt and heads off into Lassen National Forest.

Butte Creek Canyon was originally occupied by the Maidu, but they were quickly expelled from their homes when gold was discovered along the Centerville Road, about two miles past the covered bridge. Watch for mine tailings in the creek. Butte Creek Canyon is at the far end of Gold Country; a fair amount of gold was taken from the creek.

The Centerville Road can be traveled on pavement for about five more bucolic miles past the covered bridge and up the main branch of Butte Creek Canyon, passing an occasional meadow and then crossing the creek on a temporary bridge (the beautiful 1907 Centerville Bridge was destroyed in a truck accident in 1997). Just beyond the temporary bridge is the former site of the town of Centerville, which, along with nearby Bonyard Flat (Chinatown), Helltown, Whisky Flat, and Paradise Flat, sprang up during the gold rush and went away when gold fever cooled.

Though the towns are gone, the excellent Colman Museum next to the 1894 Centerville School documents the history of the canyon, and is open on weekends in the afternoon. Beyond Centerville, the dirt road twists and turns, passing by the Centerville Cemetery to eventually reach the head of the canyon at Nimshew Road and, just beyond, the Skyway, more than ten miles above Paradise.

There are many paths to Paradise. I found mine long ago at the bottom of Butte Creek Canyon.

PART VIII

WINE COUNTRY

My final journey took me to the North Bay counties, to the heart and soul of wine country, in and around the valleys of Napa and Sonoma. California's wine country embodies many of the wonderful elements found across Northern California: vast agricultural valleys, rugged mountains, and historic cities and towns. There are some unusual features, too, including a petrified forest and roaring geysers.

Crowds come to the Napa and Sonoma Valleys to see the vineyards and visit the wineries along California Highways 29/128 and 12, but there's another side to wine country: Some of California's most picturesque backroads crisscross the valleys and wind up the mountains. I can't think of a better place to bring to a close my travels in Northern California.

NORTHERN SONOMA COUNTY

Most visitors to wine country arrive from one of three directions. Some come from the San Francisco Bay area to the south on busy U.S. Highway 101 or California Highway 29. Others come from the north, down U.S. 101. Still other visitors wend their way from the east, from the Central Valley, along Interstate 80 and California Highway 12.

I decided to take a less-traveled route through northern Sonoma County to wine country. This region is more remote than the southern realms of wine country. As a result, the backroads here see relatively little traffic, although the landscape is just as beautiful.

Geyserville and the Alexander Valley

One early February day, I drove across northern Sonoma County from the west, on Stewarts Point–Skaggs Springs Road, to reach U.S. 101 at the little town of Geyserville. Even before reaching wine country proper, I saw occasional vineyards clinging to the steep hillsides or growing on ridge tops along the backroad.

In autumn, the vineyards turn bright red and yellow, a spectacular display arriving just in time for the harvest. During my February visit the grapevines held no leaves, but the vineyards were beautiful nonetheless. The ground beneath the craggy vines was carpeted with yellow mustard, tiny wildflowers, and bright green grass.

Stewarts Point–Skaggs Springs Road ended where Dry Creek Road began, less than a mile from U.S. 101. A left turn from Dry Creek Road onto Canyon Road took me across U.S. 101 to quiet California Highway 128 and Geyserville, in the fertile Alexander Valley, named for Cyrus Alexander, who settled the area in 1841.

Geyserville contains a few blocks of historic buildings, including the Bosworth and Son general store, which was crowded with goods from floor to ceiling. I met the founder's grandson and current store owner, Harry Bosworth, who told me the building was constructed in 1903 and originally

FACING PAGE:
WILD MUSTARD UNDERSCORES THE ROWS OF VINEYARD TRELLISES ON A WINTER MORNING IN THE NAPA VALLEY.

INSET:
WINE AGES FOR TWO YEARS IN SIXTY-GALLON FRENCH OAK BARRELS THAT LINE THE CELLAR AT THE MAYACAMAS WINERY.

housed a buggy shop and a mortuary. The building became a general store in 1911. True to its heritage, Mr. Bosworth's store sells everything from cowboy hats to cemetery plots.

After saying goodbye to Mr. Bosworth, I headed east on Highway 128. I crossed the Russian River, named for Russian explorers who built Fort Ross on the damp Pacific coast of what would become Sonoma County, in 1812. The Russians, who departed Northern California in 1842, planted vineyards in California with grapevines believed to have come from Peru. In 1846, Cyrus Alexander planted his own vineyards with vines he acquired from the abandoned Fort Ross.

A Visit to Devil's Canyon

Pine and oak clad mountains rose before me, and vineyards bordered either side of Highway 128. The highway veered to the southeast and, about four miles past Geyserville,

reached Geysers Road. I turned left and began a sixteen-mile drive up a winding backroad into the Mayacamas Mountains.

I soon had spectacular views of the Alexander Valley. Farther up the mountain I saw a hand-painted sign at the end of a driveway that read "Mercuryville—Pop. 2—Half Mile High." I might have made a detour here to meet the population of Mercuryville, but a second sign said "No Trespassing."

I reached a junction with Geyser Resort Road, which took me into Devil's Canyon, where a resort catering to the wealthy opened in the 1850s. The resort burned down in 1937, and in the intervening years all traces of the buildings have been removed. Today, the resort has been replaced by twenty-two geothermal power stations that convert steam from the hot springs—called The Geysers—into electricity. The Geysers are scattered across the hillsides of

THE GOLDEN COLOR OF AUTUMN HOLDS SWAY OVER VINEYARDS, ALONG HIGHWAY 128, IN WINE COUNTRY.

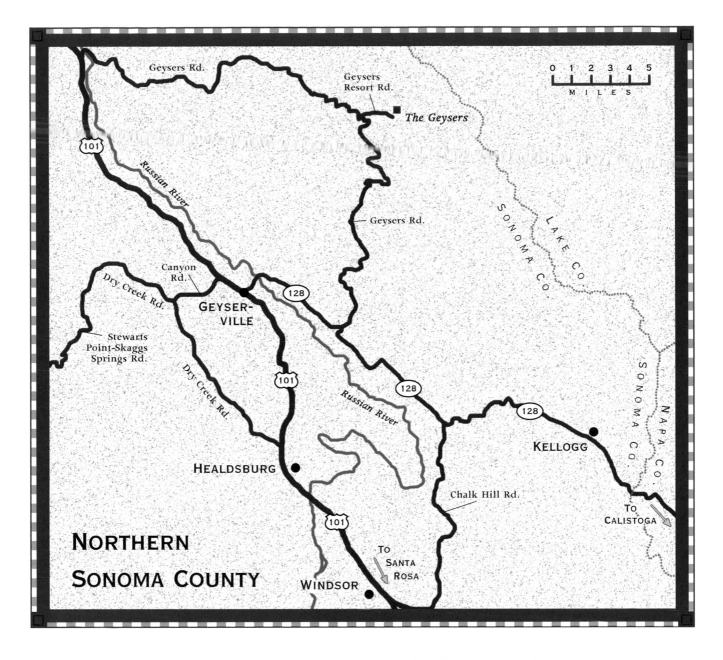

NORTHERN

SONOMA COUNTY

Devil's Canyon, and they produce more electricity than any other geothermal field in the world.

Visitors are not allowed past a guard booth at the entrance to Devil's Canyon. But you can see a few of the power stations from the road, including giant plumes of steam rising from the tops of buildings the size of airplane hangers that enclose the geysers.

I was a bit disappointed not to have a close-up look at The Geysers. And I was little sad, too, that the landscape around this intriguing natural phenomena has been so drastically altered. I felt better as I began driving down the mountain and took in the

beautiful view and realized that on this backroad the journey was as important as the destination.

Although I could have stayed on Geysers Road for sixteen more miles to reach U.S. 101 north of Geyserville, I returned to Highway 128 the way I had come and continued through the Alexander Valley.

At the southern end of the valley, Highway 128 twisted east, through a narrow pass in the Mayacamas Mountains. I entered Knights Valley, named for pioneer William Knight, who settled the valley in the 1850s. The land in Knights Valley was initially free of vineyards; pastureland was speckled with

oak trees. As I drove past Kellogg, a community of a few homes and barns, I could see Mount St. Helena to the northeast, 4,343 feet above sea level.

Coming around a bend, I plunged back into a landscape filled with vineyards. Highway 128 climbed out of Knights Valley to slice through a low point in the Mayacamas Mountains and crossed from Sonoma County into Napa County and the northern end of the Napa Valley.

THE NAPA VALLEY

Just thirty miles long and no more than five miles wide, the Napa Valley and its principle highway are often crowded with visitors. Even so, there are many quiet backroads to explore.

Napa, in the language of the Wappo tribe which once inhabited Napa and Sonoma Counties, means "land of plenty." Today, the name is apt, as the picturesque valley and the surrounding mountains are home to dozens of vineyards producing bountiful grapes and a dizzying array of vintages. But entrance into the Napa Valley brings the traveler into a region known for more than just its fine wines. The Napa Valley is also home to picturesque towns and magnificent collections of art, geysers and dormant volcanoes, the Hubcap King and Seventh-Day Adventists.

The Hot Springs of Calistoga

Via Highway 128 from northern Sonoma County, I reached Calistoga, a resort town known as the "Hot Springs of the West." Native Americans were the first to ameliorate their physical ills in the hot springs that dot the area. Many of Calistoga's naturally heated pools have been turned into spas, where visitors partake in the corporeal pleasures of mud, mineral, and steam baths.

Calistoga's quaint downtown is located east of Highway 128, along Lincoln Avenue, which is also Highway 29. Beginning as a

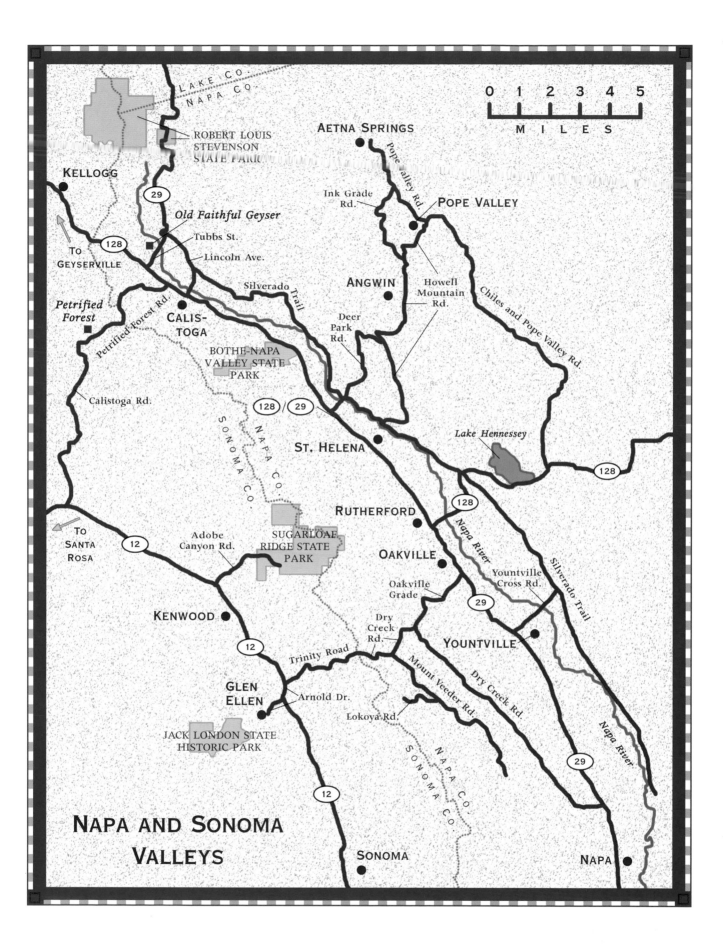

NAPA AND SONOMA VALLEYS

Lake Co.
Napa Co.

ROBERT LOUIS
STEVENSON
STATE PARK

AETNA SPRINGS

KELLOGG

29

Old Faithful Geyser

Tubbs St.

128

TO
GEYSERVILLE

Lincoln Ave.

Pope alley Rd.

POPE VALLEY

Ink Grade
Rd.

Silverado Trail

ANGWIN

Howell
Mountain
Rd.

Chiles and Pope Valley Rd.

Petrified
Forest

Petrified Forest Rd.

CALIS-
TOGA

Deer
Park
Rd.

BOTHE-NAPA
VALLEY STATE
PARK

Calistoga Rd.

128 / 29

Lake Hennessey

Sonoma Co.
Napa Co.

ST. HELENA

128

TO
SANTA
ROSA

12

Adobe
Canyon Rd.

SUGARLOAF
RIDGE STATE
PARK

RUTHERFORD

128

Napa River

OAKVILLE

Yountville
Cross Rd.

Silverado Trail

KENWOOD

Oakville
Grade

29

12

Trinity Road

Dry
Creek
Rd.

YOUNTVILLE

Dry Creek Rd.

GLEN
ELLEN

Arnold Dr.

Mount Veeder Rd.

Lokoya Rd.

Napa River

JACK LONDON STATE
HISTORIC PARK

Napa Co.
Sonoma Co.

29

12

SONOMA

NAPA

MILES
0 1 2 3 4 5

real estate venture that was to rival the health spa in Saratoga Springs, New York, Calistoga was inadvertently named by Sam Brannan, the apostate Mormon who became California's first millionaire. According to local legend, Brannan was to christen his project "the Saratoga of California" at a dinner party. But Brannan, his tongue relaxed by drink, reputedly pronounced it "the Calistoga of Sarafornia."

I had a good cup of coffee at the Calistoga Roastery and then stepped across Lincoln Avenue to Nance's Hot Springs. Bob French, the attendant who takes able care of the patrons on the men's side of the mud and mineral baths, graciously showed me the system of tanks and pipes that supply hot water to a row of mud tubs and bathtubs. He took me to the back of the building, where tanks and pipes collected and channeled hot mineral water. Mr. French opened a valve on a pipe, and for a few seconds a horizontal pillar of hissing steam indicated the great power of the geyser behind the whole operation.

THIS WAY TO NANCE'S HOT SPRINGS IN CALISTOGA.

I left Mr. French and moved on to the Sharpsteen Museum, which displays historically accurate dioramas of Calistoga as it existed in its early days. Then I cruised by the Brannan Cottage, the last of the original resort cottages built by Sam Brannan in 1859. The site of the Brannan Store, the first commercial enterprise in Calistoga and now a private residence, was just up the street. In its heyday, the Brannan Store reputedly took in fifty thousand dollars in one year, a princely sum in those days.

I drove north a mile or so to Tubbs Street and the Old Faithful Geyser, Calistoga's answer to the geyser of the same name in Yellowstone. The Calistoga version usually roars to life about every hour or so. The geyser is on private property and there is a small fee to watch the eruption. On my visit the geyser erupted about every ten minutes, its cycle speeded up by extra water flowing underground after a recent rainstorm. With Mount St. Helena serving as an imposing backdrop, I watched the water and steam shoot more than fifty feet into the air.

That night I stayed at The Elms, an elegant and comfortable bed-and-breakfast. After breakfast the next day I took to the road again to explore the southern reaches of the valley as well as the country to the east.

Highway 128 was already clogged with cars and busses, and the sidewalks in Calistoga were teeming with pedestrians this late Sunday morning. The congestion would grow heavier the farther south I traveled. I sensed it was time to find myself a backroad.

St. Helena

I drove about a half mile up Lincoln Avenue to the Silverado Trail. This lovely alternative to Highway 128 carried me past vineyards and wineries along the east side of the valley. About ten miles south of Calistoga I turned right onto Deer Park Road and reached Highway 128, which now ran concurrently with Highway 29. I was at the northern edge of downtown St. Helena, near the renowned Beringer Vineyards. Frederick Beringer and his brother Jacob founded the winery in 1876, and it has been up and running ever since (during Prohibition, Beringer still produced wine, including li-

censed wine for religious purposes), making it the oldest continuously operating winery in the Napa Valley. It was also the first winery to offer tours of the premises, including the imposing Rhine House mansion, once home to Frederick Beringer and now the gift shop and wine tasting center.

Back on the road, I gritted my teeth and drove, along with too many other cars, about two miles north on Highway 29/128 (also signed as Main Street in St. Helena). My reward for putting up with the traffic was a stop at the Hurd Candle Factory, where beeswax candles are formed by hand. A mile or so to the north of the candle shop I stopped at the Bale Grist Mill State Historic Park. A two-minute walk from the parking lot brought me to the restored mill and granary, which were originally constructed with local redwood and Douglas fir in 1846, by Dr. Edward Turner Bale. The slow grinding of the mill reputedly gave ground corn and wheat a special quality, good for making local specialties, including corn bread, yellowbread, shortening bread, and spoon bread.

I also traveled a few miles farther north and visited two more wineries. At Stonegate

I photographed wooden casks sitting in the late afternoon sun. And at the elegant Clos Pegase Winery, I admired the whimsy of noted architect Michael Graves, who designed a Grecian-like "temple of wine." For inspiration, Graves drew on the ancient Palace of Knossos on the Mediterranean island of Crete. Several contemporary, monumental pieces of sculpture grace the grounds of the winery. Inside, the tour took me past collections of art and wall-sized murals and into the 20,000-square-foot cave that holds some 4,000 barrels of wine.

Back in downtown St. Helena, I stopped by the charming Napa Valley Olive Oil Manufacturing Company, on Charter Oak Avenue. The store, on the south side of town, has been owned and operated by the same family since 1930. Olive oil is no longer manufactured in St. Helena, but the original equipment used to crush and press the olives is displayed next to sausages, cheeses, and wines for sale. I watched Leonora Particelli total customers' purchases by hand on butcher paper, the way it's been done since the store first opened.

Yountville

Bypassing Highway 29/128 once again, which now was also called the St. Helena Highway, I took Pope Street east, and returned to the Silverado Trail heading south. Four miles from St. Helena, I crossed Highway 128, which had broken away and veered east from Highway 29 at the town of Ruth-

LEFT:
THE EXTRAVAGANT, A SCULPTURE BY FRENCH ARTIST JEAN DUBUFFET, GRACES THE GROUNDS AT THE ELEGANT CLOS PEGASE WINERY.

ABOVE:
A COLORFUL FIELD OF TRELLISES AWAITING NEW VINES ALONG HIGHWAY 128.

LITTO'S HUBCAP
RANCH ALONG POPE
VALLEY ROAD.

The Pope Valley

But my route this day kept me well north of the city of Napa, where the pace of life is slower and vineyards are interspersed with ranch houses and pastureland.

From Yountville I once again took the Silverado Trail, this time retracing my way north to Highway 128. A right turn onto Highway 128 took me toward Lake Hennessey through a narrow canyon filled with oaks and pines. A pipeline carrying water from the lake to the Napa Valley vineyards was soon visible on my left. The canyon broadened, the road began to climb steeply, and when it leveled out I found myself driving along the south side of Lake Hennessey. The oaks along the road were hung with Spanish moss and mistletoe; pine trees topped the ridges surrounding the lake.

Highway 128 continued east toward Lake Berryessa, but I turned just beyond Lake Hennessey, onto Chiles and Pope Valley Road. After a few miles the road climbed into long, narrow Chiles Valley, where the roadway was lined with oaks; the open land behind the trees was a mix of pastureland and young vineyards. The valley is named for pioneer Colonel Joseph Ballinger Chiles, who arrived in California by wagon train in 1841. Chiles built the first American flour mill in Northern California, near Lake Hennessey.

At the end of Chiles Valley, the road traveled into the hills and, a dozen miles from Lake Hennessey, dropped into Pope Valley, named for pioneer Julian Pope. Pope, who spent a year in a San Diego jail for crossing into Mexico without official permission, stayed in California after serving his time and ultimately obtained a land grant in the future Pope Valley from the Mexican government in 1841.

Chiles and Pope Valley Road ended at the little town of Pope Valley, where there was a country market and an auto repair garage, but no gas station. I had a pleasant conversation with Elgie Kirkpatrick, who operates the garage with her husband and son. Elgie's

erford. I stayed on the Silverado Trail, and in another five miles, I reached Yountville Cross Road and turned right to cross the Napa River and enter little Yountville, named for the first American to settle the Napa Valley, George Calvert Yount. Born in North Carolina in 1794, Yount received a land grant from Mexico in 1836. He built a log blockhouse, an adobe home, a gristmill, and a sawmill, all of which have disappeared. But Yount's namesake town remains, with shops, wineries, a country market, and the Napa Valley Museum, which opened in 1998 and features exhibits on local history and the wine industry.

Past Yountville, Highway 29 continues as a four-lane highway to Napa, the largest town in the valley. The backroads of wine country end at Napa, the vineyards displaced by a more urban setting. But Napa, the county seat, is not without charm. The town boasts a number of Victorian homes and has a pleasant, old-fashioned downtown. The Napa Valley Wine Train departs daily from the town depot, chugging along the tracks to St. Helena and back.

grandfather, Tom Neal, opened the garage in 1912.

Continuing north on what was now called simply Pope Valley Road, I passed Ink Grade Road on my left. Another mile brought me to Litto's Hubcap Ranch, where I met Kelly Damonte. Kelly told me that her father-in-law, Emanuele "Litto" Damonte, over some thirty years until his death in 1985, decorated his house, fences, and driveway with two thousand chrome hubcaps. The elder Damonte, known as the "Hubcap King of Pope Valley," can rest easy in his grave, for Kelly and Mike (Kelly's husband) have continued to decorate the ranch with a steady crop of shiny chrome.

I returned to Ink Grade Road, now on my right. This narrow, twisting road is named for pioneer rancher Theron H. Ink, whose beautiful family home, the Ink House, is now a bed-and-breakfast that graces the town of St. Helena. The Ink Grade Road traveled up through a forest thick with Douglas firs, moss-covered oaks, and even the occasional redwood, on the west side of Pope Valley. Views into the valley were occasionally splendid, but more often than not my view was hemmed in by the trees.

At the top of a ridge I reached White Cottage Road, and just beyond it, I turned right on Howell Mountain Road and headed downhill toward the Napa Valley. In a few minutes I reached the little Seventh-Day Adventist community of Angwin. I briefly explored Pacific Union College, which is part of the Seventh-Day Adventist church; sixteen hundred students attend classes on the pretty, two-hundred-acre campus. Many of the buildings were originally part of the Angwin Resort, built by Edwin Angwin, a local land owner, in the late 1870s; the resort's hotel, cottages, and even the bowling alley are now classrooms and dormitories.

Past the college, Howell Mountain Road brought me to a junction with Deer Park Road, which I took. After several switchbacks and a few more miles, I reached the

junction with Glass Mountain Road, on my right, which leads to Elmshaven, the Victorian mansion occupied at the turn of the last century by Ellen G. White, one of the founders of the Seventh-Day Adventist religion. But I continued on Deer Park Road and soon returned to the Napa Valley floor. Rather than spend the night in a bed-and-breakfast, I camped that night in nearby Bothe–Napa Valley State Park, surrounded by oak trees and ferns. In February, I almost had the campground to myself.

Oakville

I awoke to an overcast morning; it looked like rain was coming, so I thought it might be a good day to spend some time in a wine cellar. Not all the wineries in the Napa Valley are in the lowlands; many others, less frequently visited, can be found along the backroads in the surrounding mountains. I resolved to use this day to visit just such a vineyard.

I drove from the state campground to Oakville, a tiny community just south of Rutherford. I stopped in the town at the popu-

OLD AND UNPRODUCTIVE VINES ARE BURNED EACH WINTER IN WINE COUNTRY. THIS PILE WAS SET ABLAZE OFF HIGHWAY 29 NEAR THE OAKVILLE GROCERY.

MASSIVE OAKS ALONG
MOUNT VEEDER ROAD,
ON THE WAY TO THE
MAYACAMAS VINEYARDS.

lar Oakville Grocery, built in 1881, where I purchased a smoked turkey sandwich and packed it away for a picnic later in the day. Then I drove south for a third of a mile on Highway 29 and turned right onto the road known as the Oakville Grade. I stopped to watch a winter wine country ritual, the pruning and burning of old and unproductive vines. I got out of my car and walked close to the fire, and on this cold day the heat coming off the flames felt good.

Into the Mayacamas Mountains

The Oakville Grade led me up and down the eastern slopes of the Mayacamas Mountains. About three miles from Highway 29, the Oakville Grade ended at a junction with Dry Creek Road, which now took over the chore of taking me farther into the mountains. About a half mile west of the junction I turned left on Mount Veeder Road and drove through a forest of enormous oaks and occasional redwoods.

I continued about three miles through the forest before turning right on Lokoya Road, named for the Native American tribe that once lived on the slopes of Mount Veeder. Another half mile up the mountain on the steep road brought me to the Mayacamas Vineyard's dirt driveway, on my left, which was even steeper than Lokoya Road. A half mile later I found myself at the Mayacamas Vineyards, on the lip of a dormant volcanic crater near the summit of Mount Veeder.

While many wineries in Napa and Sonoma Counties are open everyday for visitors, others like Mayacamas require prior reservations. I had called ahead and set things up at Mayacamas, so I knocked on the door of the 1891 stone winery building. Trina Wagner, the winery manager, opened the door and joined me outside for a pleasant tour under the somewhat trying conditions of the rain that had finally arrived. We looked out from under umbrellas at the fifty-two acres of vineyards, which grow on steep, rocky slopes and run down to the edge of the thick evergreen forest that chokes the bottom of the crater.

Trina told me Mayacamas produces about five thousand cases of wine a year, a relatively small amount. She said the vineyards at Mayacamas produce small crops of tiny, favorable grapes. Given the beautiful, isolated surroundings of the winery, and the quality of the wines that are produced there, it's not difficult to see why the owners, Robert and Mary Travers, think small is beautiful, and do not intend to expand the vineyards or the winery.

My guide took me into the cool wine cellar, where Cabernet Sauvignon, Pinot Noir, Chardonnay, and Sauvignon Blanc wines were aging in wooden barrels and casks. During the harvest season, the grapes are crushed and destemmed, and the mash spends one to two weeks fermenting before it's purified and stored for two years in large American oak casks. Then the wine is drawn off and divided into sixty-gallon French oak barrels, where it ages another year. Before Mayacamas releases the wine for sale, it spends two more years in bottles.

Now it was time to go. As I looked outside and pondered the rain, Trina told me more than sixty inches of rain can fall on the vineyards over the course of the year. It seemed like most of that sixty inches was falling today, but the rain began to lessen as I drove down the muddy, dirt road toward the Sonoma Valley.

THE SONOMA VALLEY

The Sonoma Valley is hemmed in by the Sonoma Mountains to the west and the Mayacamas Mountains to the east. Often referred to as the Sonoma Valley, but officially known as the Valley of the Moon, the valley is home to world-famous wineries, the one-time residence of author Jack London, and the site of an "independent" California under the Bear Flag Republic.

Jack London and Sonoma

I drove back to Dry Creek Road and turned left. The road continued to climb, and I crossed into Sonoma County. Here Dry Creek Road assumed a new name, Trinity Road. I crested the mountains, and the beautiful Sonoma Valley and rugged Sonoma Mountains were visible before me.

Cavedale Road took off from the left on a longer, winding route to the valley. But I followed the more direct Trinity Road to Highway 12. Trinity Road ends at the intersection with the highway, and I suddenly found myself on the valley floor, with Kenwood and Santa Rosa to the north, and the city of Sonoma to the south. I turned south and a mile or so later came to Arnold Drive, where a right turn brought me to the little town of Glen Ellen, named in 1869 for the wife of Charles Stuart, the town's founder.

Glen Ellen and environs is Jack London country. Born in San Francisco in 1876, London hunted seals aboard a sailing ship in the Pacific and traveled around the United States as a hobo. His wanderlust temporarily sated, he returned to the Bay Area to finish high school, but didn't stay put for long after that.

JACK LONDON, AUTHOR OF *THE CALL OF THE WILD*. (COURTESY OF CALIFORNIA STATE LIBRARY)

He spent the winter of 1897–1898 in the Yukon during the Klondike Gold Rush, though he didn't find the bonanza he sought—at least not yet. Upon his return to California, he began to see writing as a way to escape the hard, physical labor that he thought would be his lot in life. Drawing on his experiences in the far north, he started to write stories, and it was in 1903 that his book *The Call of the Wild* catapulted London into fame and fortune. London had

discovered a mother lode of a wholly different sort.

London, an early environmentalist, settled in the Sonoma Valley in 1905. He married his first wife, Bess Maddern, not so much because he loved her, but because he believed she would bear him strong children. Indeed, the couple had two daughters. But when London met Charmain Kittredge, who was five years his senior, he divorced his wife and married what London described as his "Mate Woman." The couple traveled the world together, but felt most at home in the Sonoma Valley. London died of renal failure on his ranch in 1916, at the age of forty.

Glen Ellen has a Jack London bookstore, a gift shop, and a saloon. Jack London State Historic Park, which contains much of London's ranch property, lies just east of town. I ate the sandwich I'd purchased from the Oakville Grocery while sitting on the front porch of the cottage where London did much of his writing, and I visited the ruins of Wolf House, London's palatial home that burned the night construction ended.

I returned to Highway 12 and drove south, and after a brief stop at the Valley of the Moon Winery, located on Madrone Road, I continued on to the town of Sonoma.

Alone among the cities and towns of wine country, Sonoma does not trace it's roots to American pioneers. Settled by the Spanish, Sonoma takes pride in its vibrant town square, or plaza. Reputedly the state's largest, the plaza is surrounded by historic buildings, including nineteenth-century hotels, a former Mexican army barracks, and the Mission San Francisco Solano de Sonoma. The mission marks the northern reach of the chain of Spanish outposts in California and also has the distinction of being the only California mission established under Mexican rule, after Mexico gained independence from Spain in 1821.

I also visited the home of General Mariano Vallejo, located on state park property about a half mile west of the plaza, on West Spain Street. Vallejo, a California-born Mexican, favored the Americans in the Mexican-American War and built a two-story Gothic home in 1851, moving from his adobe home on the plaza, Casa Grande. Vallejo called his home *Lachryma Montis*, or "Tears of the Mountain," likely the native Patwin name for the ample nearby springs.

Vallejo is credited with inviting Count Agoston Haraszthy, a Hungarian political refugee, to Sonoma. Haraszthy marketed the first Zinfandel wine in California; the Buena Vista Winery he built in Sonoma still stands.

California and the Bear Flag Republic

Sonoma is also the site of the short-lived Bear Flag Revolt, where American settlers declared California to be a republic on June 14, 1846. They raised a white flag in the plaza, with a single star and stripe and a crude drawing of a grizzly bear, beneath which were the words "California Republic."

The United States long coveted lands held by Mexico and had declared war on its southern neighbor a month and a day before the Americans took over Sonoma. The Bear Flag rebels were unaware of this external turn of events. By July, when U.S. forces were in complete control of California, the Bear Flag was replaced by the Stars and Stripes.

After exploring the Sonoma plaza I drove north, past Glen Ellen, to the little community of Kenwood, and turned off on Adobe Canyon Road. I followed the winding road up to a beautiful but primitive campground—pit toilets and no showers—to spend the night at Sugarloaf Ridge State Park, where there are five thousand acres of hiking and mountain biking trails.

ROBERT LOUIS STEVENSON AND THE END OF THE ROAD

I have traveled far and wide across wine country, as well as across the breadth of Northern California. But it is time for the journey to come to an end, and my final route will take me to the realm of Robert Louis Stevenson on the flanks of Mount St. Helena, overlooking the Napa Valley and the whole of Northern California beyond.

Napa Valley Honeymooners

On my last day in wine country I visited Robert Louis Stevenson State Park, on the flanks of Mount St. Helena. That morning I had driven down from the Sugarloaf campground to Highway 12 and then north to the outskirts of Santa Rosa. I took Calistoga Road back over the Mayacamas Mountains. There was a fair amount of traffic on this road. Four miles from Calistoga, I passed the entrance to the privately operated Petrified Forest, where visitors can see fossilized redwood logs. From here, the road, which was now called Petrified Forest Road, began a final, steep descent into Calistoga, and I drove east on Tubbs Street, past the Old Faithful Geyser, to Highway 29.

The vineyards gave way to manzanita, oaks, madrone, and pines as Highway 29 began to climb. There were some beautiful views of the Napa Valley as the road came to a long stretch of tight, steep hairpin curves. Seven and a half miles from Calistoga, the highway reached a crest and brought me to the small, pleasant, tree-shaded, but decidedly undeveloped Robert Louis Stevenson State Park. There was a picnic table or two, and a sign warning me to lock my car and take my valuables with me.

A trail led about a mile to the site of Silverado, which was a silver-mining boomtown in 1872. Stevenson, low on funds, enjoyed what might be described as a novel honeymoon, spending three weeks in 1880 in an abandoned miners' bunkhouse in what was already the ghost town of Silverado.

Stevenson's wife, Fanny Osbourne, was separated from her first husband and was the mother of two children when she met Stevenson at an artists' colony near Grez, France. She divorced her first husband and married Stevenson, eleven years her junior.

Stevenson sampled many of the valley's wines during his few weeks in the Napa region, and he took notes about his experiences that he would use in his later writings. He wrote about the people he met and the nascent wine industry in Napa in a memoir, *The Silverado Squatters*, published in 1883. Of course, the author is best known for writing the classics *Treasure Island, Kidnapped,* and *The Strange Case of Dr. Jekyll and Mr. Hyde.* Like Jack London, Stevenson would die at a relatively young age. He was forty-four when he succumbed to tuberculosis, while living in Samoa.

Mount St. Helena

Stevenson's honeymoon bunkhouse no longer stands, but its location along the gently graded, five-mile trail leading to the summit of Mount St. Helena is marked by a large, bronze monument shaped like the open pages of a book. I hiked a mile through oaks and pines as far as the site of the monument, but I did so with misty clouds swirling above me. Stevenson claimed that stands of redwoods once graced the airy realms above the Napa Valley and lamented that the ancient trees, having "fallen from their high estate, are serving as family bedsteads, or yet more humbly as field fences, along all Napa Valley."

Had it been sunny, occasional breaks in the forest would have allowed me views down into Lake County, to the east, and the Napa Valley, to the south and west. The summit, still four miles away, would have offered me its own majestic views. The Diablo Range would be visible to the south, where I had traveled the Mount Hamilton Road to the Lick Observatory. The Santa Cruz Mountains, with their stands of redwoods, would lie to the southwest, while the crest of the Sierra Nevada Mountains, across the intervening Central Valley, would be distinguishable far to the east. I knew the Great Basin Desert lay just beyond the Sierras.

Had I made that walk my gaze would have been drawn north, toward the Lost Coast. The Klamath Mountains would have been lost in the distance, but if it were a very clear day, I might have spied the perennially snow-capped summit of Mount Shasta, the consummate Cascade volcano, 192 miles to the northeast.

But I didn't need to make the long walk to the summit of Mount St. Helena, for I had been to all those beautiful places. They were in my photographs, and I could see them in my mind's eye whenever I wanted.

I spent a few, quiet moments enjoying the solitude at the Stevenson monument. Refreshed, I made my way down the mountain and began the journey home.

Cloud-capped Mount St. Helena rises over vineyards near Calistoga, in the Napa Valley.

EPILOGUE

I wrote, at the beginning of these pages, that this was a book of legends and myths about the land and the people of Northern California, legends and myths linked by the backroads of the Golden State. Yet, for all the stories within these pages, there are still more to be told. For every road that has been taken here, there are still more to be traveled.

But for now, it's time to pull to the side of the road, and rest a little while, before beginning the journey anew.

LEFT:
CLIFFS, CYPRESS TREES, AND THE PACIFIC, ALONG HIGHWAY 1 NEAR DAVENPORT.

FACING PAGE:
HIGHWAY 120 LEADS TOWARD THE EAST SIDE OF THE HIGH SIERRA, SOUTH OF BODIE.

SUGGESTIONS FOR FURTHER READING

AN AFTERNOON
REFLECTION IN THE
WINDOW OF THE BOONE
STORE AND WARE-
HOUSE, MAIN AND
GREEN STREETS, BODIE.

Alt, David D., and Donald W. Hyndman. *Roadside Geology of Northern California*. Missoula, Mont.: Mountain Press Publishing Company, 1986.

Bean, Walton, and James J. Rawls. *California: An Interpretive History*. 7th ed. Boston: McGraw Hill, 1997.

Beckwourth, James Pierson. *Life and Adventures of James P. Beckwourth*. Edited by T. D. Bonner. New York: Harper & Brothers, 1856. Reprint. North Stratford, New Hamp.: Ayer Company Publishers, 1986.

Burgess, Sherwood D. *The Water King: Anthony Chabot, His Life and Times*. Davis, Calif.: Panorama West Publishing, 1992.

Caughey, John, and Laree Caughey, eds. *California Heritage: An Anthology of History and Literature*. Los Angeles: Ward Ritchie Press, 1962.

Dean, J. Robert. *A Land Called California*. Del Mar, Calif.: Pacific Sun Press, 1979.

Dillon, Richard H. *Fool's Gold: The Decline and Fall of Captain John Sutter of California*. New York: Coward-McCann, 1967.

Eichorn, Arthur Francis. *The Mount Shasta Story*. Mount Shasta, Calif.: Mount Shasta Herald, 1957.

Farquhar, Francis P. *History of the Sierra Nevada*. Berkeley: University of California Press, 1965.

Gillenkirk, Jeff, and James Motlow. *Bitter Melon: Inside America's Last Rural Chinese Town*. Berkeley: Heyday Books, 1993.

Heizer, Robert F., and Albert B. Elsasser. *The Natural World of the California Indians*. Berkeley: University of California Press, 1980.

Heizer, Robert F., and Theodora Kroeber, eds. *Ishi the Last Yahi: A Documentary History*. Berkeley: University of California Press, 1979.

Mason, Jack. *Earthquake Bay: A History of Tomales Bay*. Inverness, Calif.: North Shore Books, 1976.

Nelson, Byron. *Our Home Forever: The Hupa Indians of Northern California*. Salt Lake City: Howe Brothers, 1988.

Rawlings, Linda, ed. *Dear General: The Private Letters of Annie E. Kennedy and John Bidwell, 1866-1868*. Sacramento: California Department of Parks and Recreation, 1993.

Sanborn, Margaret. *Yosemite*. Yosemite, Calif.: The Yosemite Association, 1989.

Schoenherr, Allan A. *A Natural History of California*. Berkeley: University of California Press, 1992.

Seagraves, Anne. *Women of the Sierra*. Lakeport, Calif.: Wesanne Enterprises, 1990.

Wilson, Jim, Lynn Wilson, and Jeff Nicholas. *Wildflowers of Yosemite*. Yosemite, Calif.: Sunrise Productions, 1987.

INDEX

ABOUT THE AUTHOR

David M. Wyman is a freelance writer and professional photographer based in Los Angeles. Dave owns and operates Image Quest, a natural history and photography tour company that conducts trips to California wilderness areas. He directed the travel photography and wilderness outings programs at the Unitversity of Southern California for almost fourteen years. A former reporter and photographer for the *Willows Daily Journal* in Northern California, Dave has also published articles and photographs in *Backpacker, Outdoor Photographer, Outside,* and *Westways. Backroads of Northern California* is his first book.

PHOTOGRAPH BY DAN AVILA